מכתב ברכה מאת הגאון האמיתי שר התורה
מורינו ורבינו מרן יעקב יצחק הלוי רודרמן זצ"ל

RABBI JACOB I. RUDERMA
400 MT. WILSON LANE
BALTIMORE, MD. 21208

D1563929

יעקב יצחק הלוי
באלטימאר 2

נעים לי מאד למלא בקשת תלמיד ישיבתנו לשעבר הרב יצחק
לאענברון נ"י ולכתוב איזה שורות של ברכה לתנועת הנוער
N.C.S.Y. שהוא עומד בראש אחד הסניפים. והנה עבודתם
הברוכה של מדריכי תנועה זו ידועה לי מכבר. מי ימלל גבורת
עוזם שמשימים לילות כימים במסירה אבהית למען ילדים
שבעוונותינו מספיקים בילדי נכרים ורחוקים מרוח ישראל סבא,
והצלחתם הגדולה ידועה אשר מספר ניכר של תלמידים
הלומדים כיום בישיבות היתה התחלת צעדיהם בדרך התורה
והיראה על ידי תהנועה החשובה הזאת. תחזקנה ידיו וידי
העוזרים עמו ויזכו לראות פרי עמלם ויבוא עת שיאמר לציון
רוחמה ולכל אחד יאמר עמי אשר בך אתפאר.

יעקב יצחק הלוי רודרמן

It is with great pleasure that I fulfill the request of a past student of our
Yeshiva, Harav Yitzchok Lowenbraun, let his candle burn bright, and write a
few lines of blessing and encouragement to the youth movement, NCSY, of
which he is a Regional Director.

The blessed work of the leaders of this movement is well known to me
already. Who can give proper praise to their mighty strength? They make
their nights into days in fatherly devotion in behalf of youth who, due to our
many iniquities, are content with foreign ideas and philosophies and are distant from the spirit of our ancestor, Israel. Their great success is known in
that a substantial number of students who learn in Yeshivos today took their
first steps in the way of Torah and righteousness through this important
movement.

MAY HIS HANDS AND THE HANDS OF HIS SUPPORTERS BE STRENGTHENED.

May they merit to see the fruit of their labor, and let the time come at
which "Zion will be called 'She who received compassion ...'" "And unto
every one would be said, 'This is my people in which I glory.'"

The overwhelming majority of Jewish youth in America are not able to read this volume with any kind of meaningful comprehension!

This is a tragic situation and its cause, "Jewish illiteracy," is at the root of all the problems that **NCSY** faces every day on the battlefield for Jewish Survival.

When it comes to Jewish topics, our youth do not even understand English, let alone Hebrew.

A communication gap exists between those who have a strong sense of Jewish identity and the others whose sense of Jewish identity can be charitably described as anonymous.

NCSY has successfully bridged this gap by pulling thousands of our youth out of the abyss of assimilation.

We need your support to increase our efforts against the tidal wave of ignorance that has engulfed our young people.

Remember:
The Jewish People of Tomorrow
Are the Jewish Children of Today

This publication is dedicated

in memory of

Rebbetzin Frieda K. Hirmes ע׳׳ה

A true Aishes Chayil
whose life was an inspiration
to her children and grandchildren.

by Mrs. Hannah Storch and Family

The Facts on NCSY

NCSY began nationally in 1954 and in the Atlantic Seaboard Region twenty-six years ago in 1961. In 1973 it emerged as a most active force, thanks to a generous grant from the Joseph Meyerhoff Fund. NCSY has grown steadily to be one of the largest and most active Jewish youth movements in the ares. Today there are more than 2,000 young people participating annulally in over 16 chapters. Among the programs we offer are:

- ☐ Outreach Programs for Alienated Youth
- ☐ Junior NCSY for ages 10-13
- ☐ Senior NCSY for ages 14-18
- ☐ Teen Torah Center (Hebrew High School)
- ☐ Summer Camp Programming
- ☐ Lave (Life and Value Experiences) Clubs
- ☐ Program and Curriculum Development
- ☐ Shabbatonim — Weekend Conclaves
- ☐ "Our Way" — Program for the Jewish Deaf
- ☐ Youth Counseling
- ☐ Community Assistance Programs
- ☐ Project Yedid
- ☐ Project Yachad for the Developmentally Disabled
- ☐ Israel Summer Seminar
- ☐ Year of Study in Israel for High School and College Students
- ☐ Scholarship Programs
- ☐ Leadership Training Programs
- ☐ Board of Jewish Education—NCSY—Hebrew School Shab- batonim
- ☐ Camp NCSY East
- ☐ Cross Country Tour
- ☐ Baltimore Jewish Basketball League
- ☐ Various NCSY Publications and Newsletters

Dedicated

In Memory of

Esther Kadish ע״ה

An inspiring woman whose memory lives
in her family's dedication to eternal ideals

ת.נ.צ.ב.ה.

— the moving force of the teshuvah movement

As an historic Torah movement for Jewish revival and return, NCSY is reversing the decaying process of assimilation and intermarriage by affecting the lives of tens of thousands of young Jews from Vancouver to San Diego... from Providence to Atlanta.

Entire communities have been strengthened and reinvigorated through the impact of the enthusiasm and devotion of young NCSY graduates for Torah study and mitzvos.

During the past twenty years NCSY has been a major force in the dramatic reversal of the direction of Torah Jewry and the reemergence and rebirth of an invigorated and expanding Torah community.

• **NCSY** pioneered and gave rise to the near miraculous phenomenon of thousands of young Jews, intelligent and accomplished searching and yearning for spirituality, Torah and roots.

• **NCSY** inspires more young people to become Sabbath observers than any other institution or program in America and Jewish life.

• **NCSY** motivates more young people each year to enter schools of Torah study on the college level than any twenty yeshiva high schools.

• **NCSY** has given rise to a special group of yeshivos in the United States and Israel for the newly observant.

• **NCSY** serves as the only outreach program in scores of American and Canadian communities.

• **NCSY** touches the hearts and minds of tens of thousands of young people each year with unique programs... such as Shabbatons, Camp Seminars, Regional and National Conventions, the Israel Center in Jerusalem, NCSY Goes to Yeshiva, Leadership Training Seminars, special periodicals, books and other publications.

• **NCSY**, one of the largest and most effective Jewish movements in the world — a powerful and effective force for Jewish survival, revival and return — urgently requires your commitment and support in order to maintain and expand its activities and programs.

The ArtScroll Series®

The Fire

by
Rabbi Hillel Goldberg

Published by

Mesorah Publications, ltd

Within

The living heritage of
the Musar Movement

FIRST EDITION
First Impression . . . September, 1987

Published and Distributed by
MESORAH PUBLICATIONS, Ltd.
Brooklyn, New York 11223

Distributed in Israel by
MESORAH MAFITZIM / J. GROSSMAN
Rechov Harav Uziel 117
Jerusalem, Israel

Distributed in Europe by
J. LEHMANN HEBREW BOOKSELLERS
20 Cambridge Terrace
Gateshead, Tyne and Wear
England NE8 1RP

ISBN:
0-89906-577-5 (hard cover)
0-89906-578-3 (paperback)

Typography by CompuScribe at ArtScroll Studios, Ltd.
1969 Coney Island Avenue / Brooklyn, N.Y. 11223 / (718) 339-1700

Printed in the United States of America by Moriah Offset
Bound by Sefercraft, Quality Bookbinders, Ltd. Brooklyn, N.Y.

To our children,

Tehilla Rivka,
Temima,
Mattis Yosef,
Shayna Ruth,
Rachel Tiferet

TABLE OF CONTENTS

Introduction
and Acknowledgments

For years I have been asked, "What is Musar?"

For years I tried to answer that question with a one-word, one-line, or one-paragraph answer.

The scope of Musar is threefold. Musar is a multifaceted Hebrew word, a time-honored genre of Jewish literature, and a particular human integrity and spirituality.

This book is meant primarily to flesh out Musar's third province—its human side.

It takes a book to provide just part of the answer to the question, "What is Musar?"

Focused as it is on Musar's human integrity and spirituality, *The Fire Within* explains how concepts were lived, more than how they were formulated. It explains the concrete more than the abstract. Better: it explains how the abstract became the concrete. It shows how individuals worked with ideas of Musar to change their lives, to transform themselves into *tzaddikim*—special Jews with exquisite sensitivity to people and heightened spirituality before G-d, *Hashem*.

I knew some of the *tzaddikim* about whom I write. I witnessed how ordinary flesh and blood used such concepts as fear of G-d (*yir'as Hashem*) and trust in G-d (*bitachon*) to become extraordinary servants of G-d. I witnessed how individuals used such techniques as "Musar prayer" and "Musar study with lips aflame" to turn theory into practice. I witnessed role models, *tzaddikim* who went beyond thinking about Musar to acting on it, bringing lofty ideals down to reality.

Theory of Musar is intrinsically valuable. It neither can nor should be wholly divorced from portrayal of *ba'alei Musar*, Musar personalities.[1] However, a unique understanding of Musar abides in the personal struggle to live it, and the personal joy that comes from it.

That struggle, and that joy, form the side of Musar to which this book seeks to serve as a definition.

Our subject matter is the Musar movement, founded by Rabbi Yisrael Salanter in Vilna, Lithuania, in the 1840s, resonating to this day in remarkable *ba'alei Musar* on several continents.

Although Musar literature stretches across many centuries in authorship and impact, rarely have Jews, in a fruitful concentration, taken this literature so seriously as to constitute a movement. One such movement was "German Pietism" (*Chasidus Ashkenaz*), in the thirteenth century. The Musar movement, begun in the nineteenth century, seems to be larger and longer lasting than German Pietism.

By now, the Musar movement has bequeathed a pantheon of *tzaddikim*, and a vision of piety, that have permanently enriched the Jewish imagination. Before Reb Yisrael Salanter, it was difficult

---

1. For an analytical review of Rabbi Yisrael Salanter's Musar theories, see my *Israel Salanter: Text, Structure, Idea—The Ethics and Theology of an Early Psychologist of the Unconscious* (Ktav, 1982).

ii

and perhaps impossible to imagine such depth of Talmudic learning, profundity of psychological insight, and perfection of human sensitivity, all in one person. I could list a similarly unique range of traits for each of the first- to fourth-generation disciples of Reb Yisrael Salanter portrayed in this book.

But let me not summarize.

That is what got me into trouble before. The definition of Musar requires its full, book-length elaboration.

One caveat: There are additional people worthy of inclusion in this book. My principle of selection is purely subjective. The people omitted are those about whom I presently do not know enough—figures such as Rabbis Yerucham Levovitz, Eliyahu Lopian, Chaim Shmuelevitz, and Moshe Chodosh.

One counsel: The non-Hebrew reader will find five Hebrew terms, especially, used repeatedly. It will help to remember them: Hashem, "The Name" or G-d; *avodas Hashem*, service of G-d; *yir'as Hashem*, fear of G-d. *Ba'alei Musar* are people who embody the ideal of Musar, who work at *avodas Hashem* from out of *yir'as Hashem*. Such people are *tzaddikim* (singular, *tzaddik*), the pious. A Yiddish term, *Alter*, "Elder," was an appelative of both affection and respect for three *tzaddikim* who were major leaders in the Musar movement: the Alter of Kelm, the Alter of Slobodka, the Alter of Novorodock.

I am indebted to many people who aided, directly and indirectly, in the preparation of this book.

First, my thanks to Rabbi Pinchas Stolper, executive vice-president of the Union of Orthodox Jewish Congregations of America, whose idea it was for me to write this book. His catalytic probing prompted a project which has brought me great satisfaction—the opportunity to record the face of Torah which Hashem has made it my lot and privilege to witness.

Of course, it took the receptivity and wise guidance of Rabbis Nosson Scherman and Meir Zlotowitz, chief editors at Mesorah Publications, to turn the idea of Rabbi Stolper to reality. My relationship with these two creative and questing publishers—as well as with Rabbi Sheah Brander—reaffirmed the outstanding reputation they have all justifiably earned.

Rabbi Nathan Bulman's generosity in sharing his vast knowledge is one of the blessings of this generation. In New York, Jerusalem, Migdal Ha'emek, and Denver, his erudition, perceptivity, and exacting standards of honesty and precision in conception and formulation taught me more than I can return. It was he, in particular, who guided me through several ideas and texts of the Musar movement—a single thread in the large tapestry of his knowledge.

With every student of the Musar movement, I owe an incalculable debt to the late Rabbi Dov Katz, author of the six-volume *Tenuas HaMusar* (*The Musar Movement*). I have drawn upon these books, and three personal interviews with Rabbi Katz, particularly in Chapters 5, 7, and 9. Personal interviews with the late Rabbi David Zaritsky, as well as his biographical novel of Rabbi Yosef Yozel Hurvitz, contributed to my understanding of Novorodock Musar. A more recent work, Yedael Meltzer's *Bederech Etz Chaim*, included a wonderfully crafted picture of Reb Shraga Feivel Frank, and I drew on this, too.

To my father Max Goldberg, of blessed memory, who first taught me to write; to my mother Miriam Goldberg (may she be distinguished for long life), whose fearlessness as editor and publisher of the *Intermountain Jewish News* is of inestimable aid to my peace of mind; to Judy Waldren, office manager of the *Intermountain Jewish News*, whose good cheer and competence turns computer code to legible copy; to Menucha Marcus, for expert technical assistance; to Rabbis Nisson and Mrs. Devorah Wolpin, and Matis and Chanah Greenblatt, whose many kindnesses over several years have not only aided, but enlightened; to the Bostoner Rebbe, Rabbi Levi Yitzchak Horowitz, whose piety has taught me new sides to Musar; to Rabbis Chaim Schneider and Chaim Yitzchak Kaplan, who provided sources and shared knowledge of Musar; to Rabbis Moshe Chait, Yitzchak Bruk, and Heschie Nekritz, who have taught me Musar by word and deed for 15 years or more; to Rabbis and Mrs. Jehiel Perr, and Naftali and Chaya Kaplan, whose careful, concerned, and considerable tutoring in Musar at early stages of my interest was indispensable (who could not learn Musar, for example, from Rabbi Kaplan's dropping everything to stay at the side of a person he hardly knew for hours—to stay at my side, as I prepared to emplane to a distant place to sit *shiva*?); and, to my esteemed teachers of Torah in Yeshiva University, Yeshiva Toras Chaim (Denver), Yeshivos Beis Yosef-Novorodock (Brooklyn, Jerusalem), and in countless corners of Jerusalem—to all of you, my profound gratitude.

A special word to my perceptive wife Elaine, whose critical reading is unerring; and to my in-laws, Mr. and Mrs. Herman Silberstein, whose dedication to Judaism, and to us, is unfailing.

I shall not express here my gratitude to the *tzaddikim* whom I was privileged to study or to witness, talk with, be inspired by. My feelings, as best I can formulate them, penetrate the chapters that now follow.

זה הספר. מתנה היא. היד זזה. העט זז. הקב"ה מאיר.
כי לעולם חסדו.
נפלאת היא. זכותי להכיר צדיקים. אם טעיתי בתאורם חלילה, משמעותי נובעת מדברי הפ"מ וז"ל ומה אעשה? עוונתי גרמו שלא זכיתי להבין דברי הש"ך בכאן עכ"ל.
עוונתי. והוא רחום יכפר עוונתי. כי קרוב הוא לקוראיו באמת. חותמו אמת. בקשתי היא לאמת. צדיקים האירו את עיני לפחות במקצת האמת.
כי לעולם חסדו.
אתה תקותי ה' אלוהים מבטחי מנעורי.

הרב הלל בן מתתיה הכהן ז"ל
ראש חדש אלול תשמ"ז

Part One: Musar Today

1.

Rabbi Binyamin Zilber

I t is the eve of Rosh Hashanah. I am impelled to write, for two reasons. First, it is this sacred and awesome season which most poignantly recalls for me images of Rabbi Binyamin Zilber. Second, I have to be impelled to write about him. I have resisted for years. I have trembled. In my mind I have begun to write about him several times, but let the project go uncompleted even in the mind, let alone on paper. I have never taken notes after meetings with him. I have never recorded what he said to me, or my impressions of being with him, or of watching him, even though I know the tricks of memory. I have trembled. I write now primarily not to recall him for others, not to convey my impressions or his words. I write mainly because I am outside the Land of Israel, the most intense location of sanctity; and the act of writing recalls him for me, summons his image, his words, his overpowering *yir'as Hashem*—fear of G-d—affording me at least something of the props with which I used to prepare myself for the holy day, in the holy land. I write primarily as an act of self-admonition, trying to give myself Musar—instruction, re-proof—that I could receive in Israel from others—most poignantly, most searingly, from Reb Binyamin.

It seems as if every moment with him is burned into my memory. I first met Reb Binyamin in Meah Shearim in 1973. I asked whether I could learn the writings of Reb Yisrael Salanter with him. He assented at once, and before I could comprehend, he was off in a rush. I quickly followed. He led me to the Novorodock *Kolel*, took an *Or Yisrael*[1] from the shelf, and we began to study.

What I was about to see then I had never seen before and doubt that I shall ever see again.

For Reb Binyamin, every word of *Or Yisrael* was sheer holiness, every utterance of Reb Yisrael a secret entrance way to the most profound levels of *avodas Hashem*, service of G-d. He recited a word, re-recited it, explained it, questioned his explanation, considered various possibilities, sat silently over it, but mostly he grasped its meaning at once, and recoiled, as if struck. The word was not the word on the page; it was the living utterance of Reb Yisrael himself. The force of its command, the depth of its penetration to the secrets of what moves men and women, and of what Hashem wishes to move men and women, moved him. It moved him spiritually, and physically. Great sighs overcame him. It took me some time to realize that he actually aspired to become a disciple of Reb Yisrael, to emulate him—not simply to revere him, to cite him, to use him to prove a point, to pledge allegiance to his importance, or his teachings—but actually to live as if he were born in earlier generations. So weighty, so laden with meaning, was each of Reb Yisrael's words for Reb Binyamin that we usually

---

1. Published by Reb Itzele Peterburger in Vilna, 1900, this contains almost all of Reb Yisrael Salanter's significant letters.

covered only a column or two in an hour. From Reb Binyamin I learned to accept Reb Yisrael as the *rebbi*, the starting point, of *yir'as Hashem* for this our own time.

Reb Binyamin was obsessed with *yir'as Hashem*; he was the living moral of all the parables I had heard about its value. Consider *yir'as Hashem* more valuable than the most precious stones, says *Proverbs*. What would I do if I were the owner of precious diamonds, sapphires, and rubies? I would treasure them, and probably touch them, hold them to the light, devote great energy to ascertaining their value. Above all I would enjoy the security of having them. I saw Reb Binyamin rushing, always rushing, to study, to pray, to keep praying, longer and longer, to deliver Musar talks, to write *teshuvos*, and, simply, to begin anew, each moment, in the search for *yir'as Hashem*. If not dashing literally, which he often was—to *shul*, or to the *beis hamidrash*, or to the the *beis ha-Musar*,[1] or to his own *beis hisbodedus*[2]—he was dashing inward, always in search. *Yir'as Hashem* needed to be guarded zealously, lest it be lost. It was a treasure, always to be touched, felt, held against the light of *Rishonim* and *Acharonim*,[3] to be tested for purity. If even slightly impure, its value diminished. It required even greater cultivation. For Reb Binyamin, there was no end to cultivation of *yir'as Hashem*, and no end to the security it provided.

Even now, when I merely imagine him praying, all the more when I saw him praying, I was—am—moved, pained, as if struck. The sense conveyed by authentic *yir'as haromemus*—awe of the Divine majesty—seemed to hover over him, through him, reaching me and embarrassing me, truly. How could I continue to cast my eyes on this? Yet I could not resist. Why could I not pray like this

---

1. A *beis ha-Musar* is a room specially designated for the study of Jewish ethical and pietistic—"Musar"—guidebooks. It is neither for prayer (like the *shul*) nor for study of Talmud (like the *beis hamidrash*).

2. A *beis hisbodedus* is a private room whose location is usually kept secret by its user. It is primarily a *beis ha-Musar*, but since it is used only by one person, often for hours or even days at a time, it is used for prayer and Talmud study as well as for Musar study.

3. The authoritative, respectively medieval and modern Talmudic commentators.

myself? Yet I tried. Why could I not retain that image in my mind's eye the year round, and not just during this sacred season? I wished so deeply that I could.

I remember one time especially, following a memorial gathering in Rabbi Ben Zion Bruk's Novorodock yeshiva in Jerusalem. An old Novorodocker, Reb Hillel Vitkind—the *darshan* (preacher) with the golden tongue—had died thirty days earlier. Many great people spoke—Rabbi Bruk, Reb Binyamin, Rabbi Chaim Shmuelevitz, and others. Then, *ma'ariv*, the evening prayer. Long after I had finished, Reb Binyamin was still praying. "A consuming fire" is how *Deuteronomy* describes Hashem. In, around, this fearer of Hashem, I could see only fire. Earlier, when he spoke, I had sensed fire, spiritual fire.

One winter day I came upon Reb Binyamin unannounced. He had said that we would study at 3:00 in the afternoon. I had assumed he meant at the Novorodock *Kolel*. He was not there. I asked where he might be, and received directions. I worked my way through the alleys of Meah Shearim, finally coming across a small, broken wooden door, hidden at the back of a worn stone courtyard. I pushed the door open, and was struck dumb, and still. There he stood, his back to me, at the lectern of a small *shul*—I later found out that he had been given the key to the *shul*, to use as a *beis hisbodedus*—he stood fully draped in his *tefilin*, weeping, and weeping. He was pouring out his soul before Hashem, about what spiritual failings I could not imagine. As I stood gazing upon something that I felt I should not see, the point was brought home searingly. A *tzaddik* is a *tzaddik* not because he is great, but because he understands, minute by minute, how small he is in relation to the only Reality that ultimately counts.

This was brought home to me with an unrelenting power as we met during the 40 days from the beginning of *Elul* until Yom Kippur. Then, Reb Binyamin's presence battered me, yanked me from my moorings, transported me to a world of purity and a level of spiritual quest far beyond my own. Reb Binyamin actually attempted to bring to life the heroic techniques of giants who, to me, were until then only historical figures.

Reb Binyamin aspired to the *madregah* or plane of Reb Itzele Peterburger, Reb Yisrael Salanter's illustrious disciple, whose dread, or *yir'ah*, during these 40 days was so overwhelming that he took upon himself not to speak, except for words of Torah. Reb Binyamin aspired to the plane of Reb Itzele. Whenever Reb Binyamin needed food, he would not tell me, but write a list. Whenever he needed a certain book, he would motion and gesture. Rarely, he would slip, utter a secular word, and then mention Reb Itzele's name with both extreme reverence and a kind of helpless musing: who can attain *his* piety today? But Reb Binyamin tried. Like Reb Itzele, he would leave his home, would remain in *hisbodedus* or seclusion in Jerusalem, in study of Torah and Musar, in *teshuvah*, in total (or near total) silence.

True to Reb Yisrael Salanter's teaching that women and men are equally obligated to study and embody Musar, Reb Binyamin admired illustrious women as well as great men. He would tell me what a privilege it was for our generation to have two such righteous women as Rebbetzin Zaks, daughter of the Chafetz Chaim, and Rebbetzin Yaffen, daughter of the Alter of Novorodock, now both of blessed memory.

So many times I visited Reb Binyamin in his home, his son-in-law's home, or in Rebbetzin Yaffen's home next to the Novorodock *Kolel*, when he drank tea. When he recited the blessing, I witnessed a *kavvanah* or intention I could summon only when praying on Rosh Hashanah. For just a one-line blessing, with no build-up through *pesukei dezimra* and *shema*, with no minyan, and no special holy time, he could summon such *kavvanah*. I felt shamed, uplifted, perplexed: whence this power to ascend?

What perplexed me equally was his capacity to communicate with me. We spoke not simply about matters of an objective nature, so to speak, matters that any competent halachic authority could address.

We spoke about deeply personal matters.

There was nothing I felt I could not share with him.

There was nothing in my background that prepared me for such a counselor; I could ascertain nothing in his background that prepared him to be such a counselor. Such measurements, clearly, were not relevant. Never once did I feel that he spoke out of defective understanding of what my soul was asking; never once did I feel that he consciously or unconsciously manipulated me in accord with some abstract notion of what people generally, as opposed to me personally, ought to be doing. From Reb Binyamin, I heard *emes*, truth—most simple, most difficult, of utterances.

Emes may be conceived as the opposite of *kavod*; truth may be regarded as the opposite of drawing attention to oneself. Reb Binyamin published many Musar books anonymously. On some of them, he announced to this effect: "Anyone who wishes may reprint this *without* permission; let the merit be his for disseminating Torah." A stumbling block in embodying and speaking truth is self-aggrandizement—projecting oneself in the public arena. To deflect *kavod* from oneself nurtures truth-seeking, and truth-telling. The conscious avoidance of *kavod* I saw in Reb Binyamin, over and over.[1] Maybe for this reason—maybe for others, too—the Chazon Ish called him "Reb Binyamin the *Tzaddik*."

Only in one context did I hear Reb Binyamin boast. He was palpably proud of his love of the Land of Israel. One summer I visited him in B'nai Brak, to find him reminiscing.

"Next month," he said, "it will be 50 years since I came to *Eretz Yisrael*. *Yovel shanim*—a Jubilee—in *Eretz Yisrael*."

He relished the words, relished what they represented.

Some months later, sadly, his wife died. I have seen strength, but rarely strength like his, at that time. I could account for it only by his attachment to *ruchaniyyus*, to spirituality. The positive force of what never left him played its role in compensating for what did leave him.

---

1. Reb Binyamin believed, however, that it was irresponsible to print a book of Halachah anonymously. His name appears on his multi-volume responsa, *Az Nideberu*, and on his other halachic works.

When I saw him three years later he dealt with the link between family and *Eretz Yisrael*. Not once in 53 years had he left *Eretz Yisrael*, he told me. He recounted the hardships during his first several years in Palestine—no water, no flush toilets, and on and on. Most clear about his recital were not the hardships, but the joy in withstanding them, in overcoming any temptation to leave or become cynical about the *Eretz Yisrael*.

"Now, anyone can come," he was saying, "but then you needed a 'certificate' from the British. Not anyone could come. It was touch and go whether you would be allowed to come." He went to his *rosh yeshiva*, or yeshiva dean: "I want to go to *Eretz Yisrael!*"

After he arrived, he and his wife raised eight children, I do not know how many grandchildren, and now he has numerous great-grandchildren, each one born, living, and studying Torah in *Eretz Yisrael*. Jewish family—Jewish future—was a *segullah*, a mysterious merit, of *Eretz Yisrael*, he was saying, citing the famous *Ramban* about merely living in Israel as constituting an overriding *mitzvah*.

That night, we spoke about various schools (*shitos*) in Musar. In explaining his own attraction to Rabbi Yechezkel Levenstein and to Kelm Musar, he said, "Our own *derech*, or orientation, is more on the side of *pashtus*, simplicity."

It struck me.

He had spoken in the third-person plural.

He had included me, as if, somehow, he and I were on the same level. I was truly complimented, and embarrassed. How I wish I could speak to Reb Binyamin tonight, the eve of Rosh Hashanah, or learn with him tomorrow, to make a last preparation to stand before the King, the Source of all uplift and embarrassment. How grateful I am that I can even summon the memories and images that stimulate the wish.

2.

Rabbi Eliezer Ben Zion Bruk

A tzaddik, somehow, affects the air, the light, the scent all around him. In entering the room of a *tzaddik*, everything changes, somehow. There is luminosity, clarity, tranquillity. To be certain, no physicist measuring the elements with the appropriate sensors could pick this up, but the change is there, real if intangible, picked up by the real and intangible Jewish soul.

How many times I stepped from a world of mundane pursuit, of evil, confusion, or disquietude, into the luminous room of Rabbi Eliezer Ben Zion Bruk, the late *ba'al Musar* and dean of the Novorodock yeshiva of Jerusalem. That room: everything in it conspired to match the illumination with which Rabbi Bruk filled it. That room: large windows opening to the east, floods of sunlight;

high ceiling, stone floor, simple book case; plain table, chairs, sofa; mostly empty, as if inviting the spirit of Rabbi Bruk to fill it.

Those evenings, in the early 1970s, when we sat together, studying the *magnum opus* of the Alter of Novorodock, a major disciple of Reb Yisrael Salanter—those evenings.

The stillness.

The silence.

The peace.

No radio, no telephone. Nothing but the voice, the aspirations, the piercing, twinkling eyes and teachings of Rabbi Bruk. For each paragraph in the Alter's work—*Madregas HaAdam (The Stature of Man)*—Rabbi Bruk knew several *aggados* or *midrashim*[1] illuminating, or illuminated by, the words of the Alter. And those words: so simple, searing, fiery, setting forth a wealth of spirit in wholehearted acceptance of *mitzvos*. I could see Rabbi Bruk struggling to purify his own simplicity into still more genuine joy, in light of the words of the Alter. I sat in awe, of course; in awe of this exquisite meeting of minds: the one dead in 1919, the other resplendently alive in making the dead *tzaddik's* words come alive, as the Sages said, "*tzaddikim*, in their deaths, are called living."

Awe, however, was but half the story—the lesser half. The example of this *tzaddik*, Rabbi Bruk, humbling himself before the teachings of the Alter of Novorodock—humbling himself and also exerting himself to grasp, to embody, these teachings—could only have the effect of making me a searcher, too.

Not simply an onlooker, in awe.

Not simply a student, a receptacle of knowledge.

But a searcher.

"All my life I have taught man to be a seeker," said the Alter. He wished neither awe nor appreciation; he wished action, from his disciples. From Rabbi Bruk—a Novorodock disciple for 50 years even then—he elicited action. Rabbi Bruk attempted not only to grasp the Alter's writings, but to act upon them, to live in accordance

---

1. *Aggadah* (plural, *aggados*) is the non-legal, historical and anecdotal literature in the Talmud. *Midrash* (plural, *midrashim*) is preponderantly non-legal commentary on the Hebrew Bible.

with the extreme joy they posited. And since Rabbi Bruk, in his essence, never simply preached—set forth ideals—but also articulated a way forward, a plan of spiritual action, he could only pull me into the process of search. He could only make me feel that I, too, had joined the Musar tradition of seeking a more pure, more genuine, experience in the life of *mitzvos*. Here, an elderly seeker had transcended generations, both forwards and backwards—back to the Alter, forward to me, a young, raw Torah student. He had created a seeker.

This was the secret of Novorodock.

This was Rabbi Bruk.

I pen these words in anguish, just a few months after Rabbi Bruk's passing. My pain, I know, he would respect, but urge me to transcend. For the great teaching of Novorodock Musar, which Rabbi Bruk embodied exquisitely, was that pain is disfiguring, even sacrilegious; and that if, for whatever reason, a person cannot transcend pain, it should not become another person's burden. A *ba'al Musar* should bear burdens privately; the world need not suffer them.

Remarkably, I saw Rabbi Bruk heave with sobs time and again on Rosh Hashanah and Yom Kippur as he led the yeshiva in prayer, but with its conclusion, I saw his countenance change, instantaneously. He was now facing not Hashem, but Hashem's creation, man. To man were due good wishes and pleasant greetings for a year of life. Anguish over spiritual failings, scalpel-like accounting with the soul, attempts to identify improper inclinations and to remedy them—these were between Rabbi Bruk and Hashem. For Rabbi Bruk's associates, there could be only hope and good cheer, not someone else's burdens.

Not to burden others is not the same as to build a shell around oneself, to hide feelings, to assume a pose. Rabbi Bruk was the most unself-conscious, open, natural person I have ever known. To be shamed by sin—truly shamed before Hashem—is to uproot all sense of shame, of embarrassment, before man. When Hashem's will alone is the criterion by which one judges oneself, there can be no psychological impediment to being open and whole with people. It is not man before whom one shudders. It is not the human appraisal which generates inner struggle to live up to a standard. Freed of games that people play, Rabbi Bruk could warmly and spontaneously welcome everyone through the window of his soul. Everything about his physicality reinforced this expectation.

How often I would sit at his table, listen to his words, and simultaneously marvel at (or be distracted by) his uncanny eyes. The pupils closed naturally to the tiniest, black pinpoints. As the absence of color, black is also the fullness of color, by virtue of the stark contrast—the clarity—that black brings to any hue in the color spectrum. Rabbi Bruk's piercing, black pinpoints brought a contrast—the clarity of simplicity—to everyone around him, everyone in his presence.

Rabbi Bruk was barely five feet tall, but in one photograph he gave the impression of being immense, like a basketball player. Especially in his later years, he appeared weak, even frail, but when he delivered a Musar talk, he gradually assumed wholly different proportions. He assumed an immensity, a power.

Just a few months before he died, I took Rabbi Bruk to deliver a Musar talk at the memorial gathering for Rabbi Yehudah Leib Nekritz (Chapter 3) on his first *yahrzeit* or anniversary of death. I had to hold Rabbi Bruk firmly as I took him to my car. He could walk only a few steps each minute. When we arrived at the *beis ha-Musar* in Meah Shearim, he had to negotiate the short distance to the lectern. When he reached it, he held it firmly, so as not to fall.

Truly he was weak.

Then, as always, he began to speak in a soft, almost inaudible voice. From the moment he began, there was silence. Everyone listened. He needed no special gesture to command respect. Gradually his voice acquired power. Before the audience knew it, and without sensing any discontinuity, the audience was listening to a loud, resonant voice, given still greater effect by Rabbi Bruk's sparse but strong gestures. That night, as always, Rabbi Bruk gestured freely.

He no longer held the lectern.

As if from nowhere, a spirit had invigorated his every fiber.

"When he came in, he looked so weak, but when he spoke, he appeared so strong," said one yeshiva student, hearing him the first time.

It was as if there were two Rabbi Bruks: the one, a small human carriage, a frail human shell; the other, a force of intellect and spirit, an intangible power of Torah-teaching which linked the image of *Elohim*, of Divine power, to the human carriage. No one ever thought of Rabbi Bruk—short, ruddy, slow—as anything but powerful.

I never saw anyone who could fully express his ideas with such sparseness of speech as Rabbi Bruk. He never gave himself to verbal excess; and of the words available to him in the dictionary, he selected only a few. Strung together with great thought and ease, deftly and definitively arranged, a few words from Rabbi Bruk collapsed entire issues into terse, stark sentences. He did not vary the vocabulary of these sentences in accord with the level of an audience. He always spoke plainly, in a way that could be taken as simplicity or profundity: he intermixed the two naturally.

Example:

A young American student asked Rabbi Bruk to comment on the ancient problem of evil: *"Tzaddik ve-ra lo*, man is righteous, yet his lot is evil" (*Berachos* 7a).

Answered Rabbi Bruk:

"It does not say, *my* lot is evil; it says, *his* lot is evil. The speaker is an onlooker. A righteous man is not an onlooker. A righteous man does not say, *'my* lot is evil.' To him, his lot is beneficence."

Rabbi Bruk's ability to convey his thoughts in the simplest, shortest sentences enabled him to communicate with potential returnees, *ba'alei teshuvah*, who usually reached Jerusalem with no Hebrew. Once they knew but a rudimentary Hebrew, Rabbi Bruk could communicate with them.

In the 1970s, three major *ba'al teshuvah* yeshivas sequentially rented space in Rabbi Bruk's Beis Yosef-Novorodock yeshiva. Of all the students in Novorodock, Rabbi Bruk was the eldest, yet it was he who best communicated with young Americans straight from hippideom, radical politics, or hedonism. There were a number of young people on whom he had a decisive influence. Some wavered, and Rabbi Bruk tipped the scales. Others, already committed, Rabbi Bruk anchored in *shivti*, a Novorodock code word for life-long committment to study of Torah.[1] Rabbi Bruk's crystalline Hebrew and palpable faith, his gentleness and holiness, willingness to listen and ruddy, sweet countenance, all had their impact.

He often found himself asked to attend the weddings of *ba'alei teshuvah*. He always went. He always met with their parents—anything to strengthen their resolve. One such individual requested Rabbi Bruk to do something a person of his stature would not normally do. Rabbi Bruk saw that to consent would be to keep open a line of communication. Several years later, when I told Rabbi Bruk that this person had married and given birth to a second child, Rabbi Bruk commented: "Every effort is worthwhile; nothing is wasted."

In the realm of the physical, too, Rabbi Bruk wasted nothing. In the Israel War of Independence, in 1948, he caught a bullet in the leg. He was hospitalized for 16 weeks. Doctors told him that only with very intensive, painful exercize could he hope to walk again.

He walked again.

He suffered several strokes. The first one left him almost totally

---

1. "*One thing I have asked from Hashem, that thing I request: Let me sit—shivti—in the house of Hashem all the days of my life*" (*Psalms* 27:4). Novorodock took "sitting in Hashem's house" to mean spending one's entire life in study of Torah. Rabbi Bruk told me that several Novorodockers who survived Siberia told him that their formal commitment to *shivti*, undertaken in the 1930s in a Novorodock yeshiva, steeled their will to survive Siberia, and to study Torah under inhuman conditions there.

paralyzed. The prognosis was bad. It was the only time I was asked not to see him. Whenever he saw someone close to him, he wept, and this weakened him. Every morning, shortly after dawn, he cried profusely, since normally he would then put on *tefilin*. The thought of being unable to stand before Hashem, to wear the sacred straps and boxes, brought him intense grief.

He refused to make peace with his new condition. First he struggled to sit up. Next, he struggled to sit in a chair, then to stand up, then, to take a step with assistance, then without assistance, until finally he could ascend the stairs again to the yeshiva.

His first stroke occurred the first of Av. That year was the first since anyone could remember that he did not deliver *Elul hisorerus shmuesn*—half-spoken, half-cried talks on the high holy days of judgment—a Musar movement tradition in Jerusalem since Reb Itzele Peterburger had ascended to Jerusalem from Lithuania more than eight decades earlier. These talks began after the afternoon prayer (*minchah*) on the Sabbath, and continued an hour past Sabbath into the blackness of night. Hundreds of Jerusalemites— Ashkenazim, Sefardim, *Chasidim, Misnaggedim*, young and old— crowded the yeshiva.

That year, the tradition was interrupted.

And yet, already by *Sukkos*, Rabbi Bruk was strong enough to deliver a Musar talk to the *ba'al teshuvah* yeshiva then located in Beis Yosef-Novorodock.

Those who had not known him before the talk could not discern a marked impediment, but it was clear from his squared-off motions that he was far from his usual health. Still, the raw power that emanated from him, the clear struggle to speak, to stand for 40 minutes and to make his points, was obvious, and overwhelming. I could see him conquering his paralysis word by word, gesture by gesture, minute by minute.

Rabbi Bruk's typically Novorodock war with nature had begun long, long ago . . .

One afternoon in the summer of 1973 he seemed particularly relaxed, even joyous. He had this way of simply radiating, just as he was, in his very being. I asked the reason for his happiness, which seemed to be on the verge of breaking into full-throated laughter. Uncharacteristically, he refused to respond. He seemed to be savoring a deep, sustaining joy that he could not easily unlock. He told me to return in two days. Then, he would tell me a story.

In two days it was 22 Tammuz, one-half century since his escape from Russia.

In that summer, the Bolsheviks had begun systematically to imprison yeshiva students. In consultation with the Chafetz Chaim, the Novorodock yeshiva dean, Rabbi Avraham Yaffen, decided to transplant the entire Novorodock network, then 600 students, from Russia to Poland.

Each yeshiva *bachur*, or student, had to decide whether to undertake a spiritual venture that a Russian or Polish border guard could abort with the flick of a trigger. Each *bachur* had to decide whether to leave home and family—perhaps forever—for the sake of Talmud study. Eliezer Ben Zion Bruk had sought permission from his parents, who agreed (as he put it) "with their will or against their will."

Young Bruk, and a few others, arrived in Minsk, the last major stopping point in Russia. They spent the fast of 17 Tammuz, a Thursday, there. On Saturday night they traveled to Koidenov, a small town closer to the border. By prearrangement, the rabbi of Koidenov gave Bruk and his comrades 20 gold rubles for transportation and bribes.

It was impossible to flee that Saturday night. On Sunday, Bruk and his group sat on an empty bench across from the rabbi's house, studying Musar with verve. Those nights they slept in a barn. Jewish townspeople were afraid to play host, lest they be caught and jailed. Finally, on Monday, the group was dressed in farmer's clothing and stuffed underneath various belongings in a wagon. The whole town bade them farewell with a blessing.

They traveled 15 kilometers in the wagon, at which point the wagon driver threw them out, saying that others would appear to take them across the border. Bruk and his friends prayed the evening prayer, *ma'ariv*, in the middle of the night. Suddenly, smugglers appeared. They all walked a short distance, then stopped. There were swamps, fields. Stop . . . go . . . They were at the border.

One of the smugglers scouted ahead.

Shots were fired.

A fire broke out.

"We are already in the world of the Holy One, Blessed be He," thought young Bruk.

The smuggler returned.

Everyone removed his shoes to avoid making the dry leaves crack. Thorns were plentiful. It was pitch black. The smuggler commanded Bruk and his friends: "Run!"

"You run too!" they replied.

They all ran.

They all made it.

Poles, awaiting them, put Bruk and friends to sleep for a few hours, then took them to a wagon. They prayed the morning prayers, *shacharis*, on the wagon, in which they traveled for 12 hours, 8:00 in the morning until 8:00 at night. Many watchmen at bridges and various gendarmes recognized them as illegals. "Great miracles rescued us," recalled Rabbi Bruk. Not once were they asked for papers.

Finally, they reached Mir, Poland, where for the first time since leaving Koidenov they received food. The next day they set out for the Novorodock yeshiva in Baranowich.

Another 24 hours in wagons.

In Baranowich, one of the escapees was called to the Torah. It was now Thursday morning, a week since the escape began. The escapee recited *birkas hagomel*, the blessing of gratitude for rescue from danger.

With this, the community understood.

Another group of idealistic teenagers had stolen across the border. A week of danger, for the sake of keeping alive the flame of Torah, was over.

But the sacrifice had only begun. Eliezer Ben Zion Bruk never saw his parents again. There was never a safe way to get back across the border for a visit. Then came the unspeakable wickedness, 1939 . . .

An iron will for Torah study, come what may—this was Novorodock.

This was Rabbi Bruk.

Only once in 13 years did I see Rabbi Bruk angry. Remarkable as it would be for most people not to lose control that long, Rabbi Bruk's anger seemed out of place. For a *tzaddik*, anger is out of place any time. In the particular incident, Rabbi Bruk was justified in the sense that he was outrageously provoked. Still, it was embarrassing.

There are several ways to cope with moral embarrassment: To become defensive, justifying oneself; to become withdrawn, trying to hide the shame; to pretend as if nothing happened; or, to lash out in further anger, trying to transfer guilt onto a provoker for causing unpleasant behavior.

Rabbi Bruk transcended the common responses. He did something else, and never was I more moved by his unself-consciousness, humility, and lack of embarrassment before man.

We were scheduled to study at 7:30 the evening of the incident, which delayed him until 8:30. When we finally sat down, Rabbi Bruk found himself in the presence of a young disciple, half-century his junior, who had witnessed everything. For me, the air was thick with unease. For Rabbi Bruk, there was neither defense nor hiding, neither pretending nor further anger. He asked me, simply, to fetch the Talmudic tractate of *Pesachim* from the shelf.

Now, Rabbi Bruk had an astonishing grasp of the vast literature of *aggadah* and *midrash*. There was never an occasion on which he could not cite just the right anecdote or adage. Usually he could cite it by heart; if not, he could locate it swiftly once he had book in hand.

That evening, he was different.

He opened *Pesachim*, but no passage presented itself. He flipped pages back and forth, but no citation flowed from his mouth. He read a while, then tried another page.

Back and forth.

This continued several minutes.

I sat in silence.

Never before had I seen Rabbi Bruk stumped. Finally, he looked up at me in a moment of sheer candor, humility, and spiritual beauty, that I shall never forget, and said:

"See, Reb Hillel, this is just what I wanted to show you. Somewhere here in *Pesachim*, it says, *'kol hako'es shocheach talmudo*, anyone who gets angry forgets his learning.'"

3.

Rabbi Yehudah Leib Nekritz

There was always something larger than life about Rabbi Yehudah Leib Nekritz.

The first time I met him, in 1968, I knew nothing of his history, his heroism, his stature. I knew nothing that should color my perception of him. Him, him alone, I confronted, naked in my conception of what a Musar personality should say or instruct, naked in any specific expectation at all, save only the hope that in his yeshiva, and in him, I would witness something of the Musar teachings—the living, present embodiment of the face of holiness that Reb Yisrael Salanter quarried from his studies of Torah and Musar.

I stood, then, before Rabbi Nekritz without questions, without quandaries, ready to see him for what he was, to hear him for what he said. And I saw someone larger than life, even as I absorbed only snatches of a conversation, its concepts so fresh, so profound.

Walking through the door of the Central Beis Yosef Yeshiva in Brooklyn, I first saw this man seated in a position I was to see for the next 16 years. He sat over a table, *sefer* or holy book in one hand, head leaning on the other hand, his large rounded chest bent over this *sefer*, his entire energy and concentration—the entire weight of his mind and mien—interpenetrating this book, as if a permanent dialogue between *sefer* and rabbi had created its own independent force, its own self-sustaining power. It was nearly 3:00 o'clock in the afternoon; the yeshiva was empty. There was only this force, this man and *sefer*—an engaged learning, a living wisdom, an illumination comprised of both the spiritual and the physical, the clarity of the *sefer* and the brightness of the afternoon light, fused in the aura of the white-haired, white-bearded Rabbi Nekritz.

I remained in the yeshiva not long, the first time; I spoke with Rabbi Nekritz not long, that cool, clear winter day. Yet I saw the essence, of both the yeshiva and the man. The *sefer*, he told me, was *Chovos Halevavos, Duties of the Heart*, by Bachya ibn Pakuda. His copy, I saw, he kept in his *talis* bag; his copy, it was clear, had been thumbed for decades. His dedication, it was equally clear, was unique. He alone was studying during those hours of rest in the yeshiva.

Dedication?

Permit me to retract. Unusual in him was how perfectly natural and unlabored was the studying, the pursuit of wisdom, the fusion with Bachya, that cast itself across the room in one unified gesture, as I first laid eyes upon Rabbi Nekritz. The teachings of Musar may be duties, philosophically speaking, they may be commandments, obligations, but to Rabbi Nekritz they were infusions of knowledge and sensitivity that he absorbed willingly, with spiritual gusto. There were like diamonds that he embraced with the will of one who has "found spoils as if stockpiled" (*Psalms* 119:162).

This I found larger than life: the ease, the naturalness, the sheer love of learning and of living the lofty lessons of Musar that, even in his gentlest gesture, suffused Rabbi Nekritz. I found it extraordinary precisely because I knew, and even could see, that his ease was not inborn.

It was built from great, unceasing effort.

I saw Rabbi Nekritz *daven*—pray—that day. Never before had I seen so clearly that prayer was an experience of reliance on Hashem, of casting burdens on Hashem, of naked acknowledgement of the finitude—and responsibility—of man.

Rabbi Nekritz in his prayer was an awesome sight.

That large carriage of his, those broad shoulders, wide chest, and firm, soldier-straight stature, bent under the weight of prayer, as if the burdens of all the world rested on him. Added to that basic posture was a very slow swaying, a very long searching of soul.

I always imagined Rabbi Nekritz carefully, thoroughly numbering off his concerns—his failures and aspirations in duties of the heart, his familial and communal requests and responsibilites, his progress and stumbling blocks in Torah study—before Hashem. I imagined all this because I never before, or since, witnessed prayer so focused, physically exhausting, and conscious of the enormity of the task; so steeped in the self-abnegating quest for mercy, so eager to accept the self-ennobling challenge of *siyyata dishemayya*, the help from Heaven.

All this I glimpsed in about three-quarters of an hour one winter day in 1968. All this I saw, over and over, as Rabbi Nekritz's smile and seriousness, fortitude and focus, diminished not one whit, all the years I knew him. He was an anchor, a magnet, a fixed point to whom disciples, family, and colleagues always turned, knowing that his steady, unruffled manner, his ever radiating wisdom and holiness, would give comfort and encouragement, just for being there.

The power of Rabbi Nekritz derived from deep spiritual wells inside him, but also from wells of spirit outside. In him I saw more than him; I saw the power of the Musar community. His was a yeshiva that was more than a yeshiva. Beis Yosef-Novorodock was a community formed in Poland before World War II, forged in Siberia during the war, and reconstituted in the United States during and after the war. Rabbi Nekritz drew his spiritual power from this community's memories, struggles, aspirations.

Everyone had his place in this community.

There was a *rosh yeshiva* or yeshiva dean, a *mashgiach* or "spiritual supervisor," and others with titled positions, though titles were of little relevance. They were awkward. Everyone in this community, in his or her own way, had the task of identifying and actualizing "his duty in his world,"[1] or her duty in her world, a task that pressed upon the consciousness with the force of Divine command, an obligation that transcended—rendered almost irrelevant—titles and positions.

Here was a community in which each participant quietly dressed himself down, struggled with self-deception and evil urges; in which each participant, without show, without fanfare, studied Musar teachings, worked at prayer, manufactured an intensity, a heat, ultimately a refined, sublime glow that gave the entire yeshiva a magnetic power—subtle, unseen, yet pervasive.

In this cauldron of purpose and spiritual pursuit Rabbi Nekritz flourished.

To this cauldron he added his gentle yet strong, inimitable leadership.

Into this community my initial encounter with Rabbi Nekritz drew me.

A Musar community bestows few honors or distinctions upon its members. Honor? This comes from Hashem, not man; the same with distinction. A Musar community makes a statement, not a request, not *please join*. It is open to all, teaches all, reaches out to all, but the request to join must spring from promptings or crises in one's own heart. Musar is an enterprise that, by definition, must be self-sustaining. This is why Rabbi Nekritz—leader, chief Musar teacher—could neither be nor wish to be more than a first among equals, student as well as teacher, taker as well as giver of

---

1. The phrase is Moshe Chaim Luzzato's at the opening of *Mesillas Yesharim*, as translated by Shoshana Perr.

inspiration, a pathbreaker but not a model. Each Musar seeker must be his own model, ultimately.

As I drew myself gradually into this community, I watched Rabbi Nekritz, but learned to be watchful, primarily, of myself. I watched those sitting around me, each person in his own location. I observed a variety of struggles, spiritual achievements, and tonalities in prayer, self-scrutiny, and philosophical approach. I learned not to aspire to imitate those sitting around me—only to appreciate their honesty before Hashem—as I began the difficult, lifelong path of discovery of my purpose in my world.

Having begun in Poland, Rabbi Nekritz's own path of discovery took a quantum leap forward, I suspect, in Siberia. He could not have done what he did there without his earlier Musar training, but I cannot imagine that the sufferings he overcame there, and the ways in which he did so, did not seal his strength and gentleness.

Here was a man, in his early thirties, suddenly deported from Poland to Siberia. His own teachers and mentors are out of reach; for all he knows, they are dead. His own Musar community is gone; for all he knows, it is destroyed. Everything is gone: kosher food, synagogues, *mikva'os*, schools, not to mention the freedom to study, or even to observe the Sabbath. There is just enough left—the barest kernel of community—to steel his fortitude and focus, to solidify his smile and seriousness. He has his wife, two small daughters, and a few comrades. True, most of the props are gone; then again, the main prop of the Musar personality is the person himself.

So it was that Siberia brought out the best, the strongest, in Rabbi Nekritz. Without *sefarim*, he continued to study, and to teach. Without freedom, he devised subterfuges to observe the Sabbath. Without *mikveh* (and in halachic compliance with all that implied), he maintained his marriage. Without schools, he educated children.

Without?

Permit me to retract.

He was not "without." He was with the opportunity to test the integrity of his Musar work on *bitachon*, reliance on Hashem. In words so simple, his reaction to the Siberian villagers reflected work—Musar work, spiritual work—on himself, so sustained.

"What did you do before you came to Siberia?" they asked.

"I was a *rebbi*, and I shall always be a *rebbi*," he responded.

"Why were you exiled to Siberia?"

"So that you would see that there is a G-d in the world, and so that we, Musarnikes, too, would see that there is a G-d in the world!"

With Rabbi Nekritz there was so much learned from so little said. He traded in phrases, not preachings; in sentences, not speeches. "From five hours of thinking, one derives five minutes of pure thought," commented Rabbi Moshe Rosenstein, *mashgiach* in the Lomz yeshiva before World War II.

Rabbi Nekritz always delivered himself of pure thought.

He contemplated and cogitated, constantly. Nothing issued flippantly from his mouth (although he, like Rabbi Bruk, was blessed with a sense of humor; he could appreciate an absurdity or discontinuity, and laugh richly). Rabbi Nekritz's simple speech represented the distilled wisdom of a steady, ceaseless search for wisdom and harmony in life, and in himself. His search gave him that wisdom and harmony. They permeated him, and his words.

Just by looking at him, by listening to him, one learned; his very being communicated balance. Analytical and questioning, he built balance from complexity, from an ability to hear both sides of a question, in life as in study. He had so much to probe in order to derive from Torah the ethical response. The deliberateness, the undisturbed manner in which he apprehended the language of life and the logic of Talmudic texts, gave him weightiness.

But the long years of practice in thinking and deliberating imparted agility and promptness of response to his weighty process of reasoning—a promptness that marked his speech, and all of his decisions, not only with profundity but with buoyancy, with *simchah shel mitzvah*, deeply rooted joy; so deeply rooted that all the rigors of exile and slave labor—the collapse of his world, of the external props—could not dent it.

Rabbi Nekritz. Rabbi Bruk. Rabbi Zilber.

A trio awesome to contemplate, wonderful to behold.

Each different, each alike.

Each shaped by one Torah tradition, Musar; each unique, individual.

Each one a fourth-generation disciple of Reb Yisrael Salanter, each one a reverberation of sanctity that testifies to the primary claim of the Torah: its Truth, as embodied in its learned and pious teachers, lives from generation to generation, teaching all of Israel, in imitation of the Holy One, Blessed be He, "the teacher of Torah to His people Israel."

These wondrous teachers of Torah, of Musar, were my guides to their own teachers and colleagues, stretching sideways and backwards, generation to generation, to Reb Yisrael Salanter himself, founder of the Musar movement.

The ways in which Reb Yisrael was able to model from the teachings of Torah on character and piety so many holy disciples—wondrous specimens of humanity, remarkable embodiments of Judaism—is the discovery to which these three exemplars of humanity, of Judaism, led me. The path of discovery is long and rich, several and single, the path of a "genius in halachah, a genius in *aggadah*, a genius in character, a genius in emotion,"[1] Reb Yisrael, son of Zev Wolf ben Aryeh, Lipkin Salanter.

---

1. "A *gaon* in *halachah*, gaon in *aggadah*, gaon in *Musar*, gaon in *regesh*"; interview with Rabbi Zvi Yehudah Kuk, 1977.

Part Two: The Musar Movement's Founder

4.

Rabbi Yisrael Salanter

"There are 70 faces to Torah" (*Osios de-Rabbi Akiva*).

It is rare that a single individual can fully illuminate even one of them.

Rabbi Yisrael Salanter was such a person. The face of Torah he illuminated is Musar, the ethical and pietistic emphasis in all literary expressions of Hashem's will—Bible, Talmud, and its commentaries. In his own life and thought, Reb Yisrael embodied the fullness of the Musar teachings, but the fullness of his achievement is larger still—the long line of his wondrous disciples.

By what criterion do we judge whether Musar—this face of

Torah—is conveyed in an absolutely authentic manner? One criterion is its capacity to perpetuate itself in accord with all the laws of the Torah. Reb Yisrael's absolute authenticity is confirmed by the *tzaddikim* he was able to generate, in a kind of ripple effect, the one generation to the next. Had Reb Yisrael not lived, it is doubtful that later generations would be heir to the precious legacies of *tzaddikim* portrayed in this book, and of other giants trained in Musar schools, such as Rabbis Aharon Kotler, Yitzchak Hutner, Yisrael Yaakov Kanievsky (Stiepler *Rav*), Yaakov Kaminecki, and Yaakov Y. Ruderman.

Reb Yisrael affected Jewish history in a manner analogous to Torah itself. As *gedolei Yisrael*[1] unveil new faces of Torah in each generation, each generation of Reb Yisrael's disciples unveil new facets in his face of Torah. Reb Yisrael was like a diamond rotated in the sun, his disciples like the rays emanating from it.

Rabbi Yehudah Leib Nekritz explained: Sabbath prayer beseeches Hashem to sustain Torah scholars "and all of their disciples *and all of the disciples of their disciples.*"

Why the prayer for *three* generations of scholars?

Rabbi Nekritz:

Authenticity in a Torah scholar cannot be absolutely verified except with the passage of time. It is one thing to be a scholar, another thing to raise up a disciple, still another to train a disciple who himself can loyally transmit what he has received—to sustain an unbroken chain of Torah tradition.

An analogy:

The smallest computational error by a space scientist will send a rocket drastically off course, but the implications of the mathematical deviation are unverifiable until the rocket has traveled a very long distance.

The smallest error in the transmission of Torah is undetectable in a great Torah scholar and perhaps even in his disciple. Further down the line, in the third generation, the true stature of the original

---

1. People whose preeminent Talmudic scholarship is more than scholarship; it is the ability to analyze personal and communal problems, and to lead. For amplification, see below, pp. 55-57.

scholar comes clear. His greatness, or flaws, are verified.

The strength of Reb Yisrael's leadership—the comprehensiveness of his integrity in Torah—is verified by his disciples' power to mold their own disciples, true to the stamp of Torah and Musar. Reb Yisrael sustained an unbroken chain of tradition. He was the conduit for an absolutely authentic insight.

Each of the Musar movement's major disciples embodied a new facet of the face of Torah that Reb Yisrael unveiled, for Reb Yisrael nurtured individuality in internalizing the experience of *mitzvos*. His disciples both perpetuated Musar and innovated within it.

We begin with Reb Yisrael—the preeminent scholar and *tzaddik*—then proceed to his disciples. We identify the one face of Torah—Musar—then turn to its luminous facets. First the diamond, then its rays.

To write and read about Reb Yisrael Salanter requires caution. As Rabbi Ben Zion Bruk forcefully pointed out to me, our casual use of words that formed the daily discourse of Reb Yisrael and his disciples robs these words of meaning. For example: *bitachon*, trust in G-d. We can trivialize it.

Reb Yisrael surely did not.

When Reb Yisrael died, his sole possessions were the clothes on his body, his *talis*, and his *tefilin*.

This was not because Reb Yisrael was "poor." In fact, wealthy laymen were so impressed by Reb Yisrael that they offered him handsome stipends to do with as he wished. They were so convinced of his indispensability to the welfare of East and West European Jewry that the guarantee of his comfort would be both personal privilege and public philanthropy.

Reb Yisrael rejected these offers. He did accept funds for communal purposes; he rejected all but the most minimal sums for himself.

An incident:

The last summer of his life, a wealthy man pressed resources on Reb Yisrael, only to be refused. Exasperated yet determined, the man sent a messenger to press Reb Yisrael to accept, at least, a new *talis* or prayer shawl. The messenger tried persuasion:

"Why, if the Holy One, Blessed be He, bestowed a small profit, the first thing I would buy would be a new *talis*."

Undaunted, Reb Yisrael replied:

"If the Holy One, Blessed be He, bestowed a small profit, I, too, would buy a *talis* first."

Reb Yisrael's response reflected the sublime level or *madregah* on which he lived. He had to feel that everything he possessed came from Hashem, not from people. "Only from *Your* hand—full, open, holy, and expansive." The essence of Reb Yisrael's Musar teaching—and, more to the point, of the way he actually lived—was to transform every act into a feeling of dependence on Hashem. He had to feel that every material item reached him from Hashem; that every observance of a *mitzvah* was an attempt to reach Hashem—to stand in His presence, to feel His infinite concern.

Only by feeling dependent on Hashem could Reb Yisrael accept anything from anybody. His would be benefactors were only potential agents of Hashem, and only he could decide whether they were meant to be actual agents. He refused the *talis* because he felt that it was offered by man. His acceptance of it would have reduced his feeling of dependence on Hashem.

Reb Yisrael did not advocate asceticism, nor did he reject the obligation to earn a livelihood. His point was that these matters should be evaluated in light of spiritual obligations generally, and of spiritual capacities personally.

This is where Rabbi Bruk's warning comes in. To be spiritually productive, we must not trivialize words such as *bitachon*. We must use the language of Musar consciously, carefully, not casually, to unfold the ethical and spiritual potential that resides in every Jew.

Reb Yisrael Salanter was born in Zagory, Lithuania, in 1810. Eliyahu of Vilna—the Vilna Gaon—died only 13 years earlier. The Gaon's great disciple, Rabbi Chaim Volozhin, founded the first major yeshiva in Eastern Europe just nine years earlier. And in

Salant, Lithuania, there lived Rabbi Chaim Volozhin's treasured disciple, the hidden *tzaddik*, Rabbi Yosef Zundel Salanter. He was called "Elijah's third mouth"—a sterling link in an unbroken chain of Torah tradition.

Reb Yisrael's father and teacher, Rabbi Zev Wolf Lipkin, was a noted Talmud scholar. He wrote commentaries on the Talmud, on Maimonides' Code (*Mishneh Torah*), and on other authoritative works. By the time Reb Yisrael was about 12, Rabbi Lipkin felt that his son needed a greater teacher.

The father's inadequacy indicated the son's genius.

In about 1822, Rabbi Lipkin sent Reb Yisrael to Salant to study with a preeminent scholar, Rabbi Zvi Broide. Rabbi Broide's wife thought it beneath her husband's dignity to devote energy to a youngster. Rabbi Broide, however, saw that this was no ordinary lad. He sent one of Reb Yisrael's early, written attempts at Talmudic creativity to world-renowned Rabbi Akiva Eiger, who termed the writings "the genius of genius." Rabbi Broide called Reb Yisrael "an *Alfasi katan*," a young miniature of the greatest early Spanish Talmudist, Rabbi Yitzchak Alfasi (*Rif*).

Judging from the mature Reb Yisrael's vast knowledge and unremitting dedication to study, the young Reb Yisrael must have dedicated day and night to study. Torah study became more than a prerequisite to observance of *mitzvos*, more than a *mitzvah* itself.

It became a key to becoming holy.

And holiness became more than the experience of Hashem's presence. It became the righting of unethical behavior, the repair of defects that caused unethical behavior.

Torah study acquired fresh connotations for Reb Yisrael through his contact with Rabbi Yosef Zundel Salanter. Soon after his arrival in Salant, Reb Yisrael began to associate with the remote Rabbi Yosef Zundel, who ultimately had a greater impact on him than Rabbi Broide.

The way Rabbi Yosef Zundel lived, it took special sensitivity to draw close to him. Despite his Talmudic scholarship, he held no official position.

And more:

He disguised himself as an ordinary householder. He did not wear standard rabbinical dress. He neither delivered Talmudic lectures nor decided questions of Jewish law.

To earn a living, he worked as a common laborer.

Almost no one knew his greatness.

He was a *tzaddik nistar*—a person who defined piety as shielding it from public gaze. Every spare moment he dedicated to Torah or Musar study.

This was the person who initiated Reb Yisrael into piety, who made him another link, another generation, in the unbroken chain of the Vilna Gaon. Molded by Rabbi Yosef Zundel in Salant, Reb Yisrael acquired the surname that remained with him the rest of his life.

Two typical incidents portray Rabbi Yosef Zundel's understanding of *avodas Hashem*, service of G-d.

Rabbi Yosef Zundel planned a trip from Salant to Vilna. He was asked to deliver a letter to Rabbi Gershon Amsterdam in Vilna, and did so.

Rabbi Amsterdam noticed that the letter came from Salant, and began to question the mailman. Rabbi Amsterdam took him to be a commoner, perhaps a peddler, as he gave no sign of distinction.

"Oh, you are from Salant," Rabbi Amsterdam began. "Do you know the great pious man (*chasid*) in Salant, Rabbi Yosef Zundel?" At mention of the word *chasid*, Rabbi Yosef Zundel began to stammer, to make light of the "pious man" in Salant.

The rabbi thought this strange.

Suddenly, he had a strange thought, and asked the mailman point blank:

"Are *you* Rabbi Yosef Zundel?"

Rabbi Yosef Zundel could honestly deny that he was a *chasid*, but not who he was. He responded affirmatively.

To which Rabbi Amsterdam responded in amazement:

" 'Hashem fulfills the will of those who fear Him!'
(Psalms 145:19). Rabbi Yosef Zundel the *chasid* wishes
Hashem to remove all sign of importance from him, that
he may be truly pious; and Hashem fulfills his will."

* * *

Young Reb Yisrael noticed that Rabbi Yosef Zundel
disappeared from the Talmudic study hall every day at the
same hour. Curious, Reb Yisrael followed Rabbi Yosef
Zundel. He watched him leave Salant, arrive at the bottom
of a hill, and wait briefly until a peddler arrived with a
heavy wagon. Rabbi Yosef Zundel joined the man in
pushing the wagon to the top of the hill, then returned to
the study hall.

There is a common lesson and different focus in each incident.
The common lesson is that to strive for piety is to shun
recognition. Rabbi Yosef Zundel believed that to attract attention,
even if only to popularize a *mitzvah* (such as assisting others), was
almost always indicative of glory-seeking or another impure motive.
And Hashem wants not only right deeds, but right motives.
The focus in the first incident (about the letter) is *bein adam
leMakom*, a deed "between man and G-d." The focus in the second
incident (about the peddler) is *bein adam lechavero*, a deed "between
man and man."
In the first incident, Rabbi Yosef Zundel sought to preserve his
anonymity, to make light of his piety, since his ultimate point of
reference was not man, but Hashem. Compliments only pained him,
as they could divert him from the progress he still had to make
in *avodas Hashem*. In the second incident, Rabbi Yosef Zundel
projected *bein adam lechavero*—dedication to humanity—even as
the privacy of his dedication added a spiritual element; even as his
willingness to do a favor (deliver a letter) added an ethical element
in the first incident.
Musar connects *bein adam leMakom* and *bein adam lechavero*,
devotion to Hashem and humanity. Devotion to Hashem means

doing favors for His precious creation, man. Devotion to humanity means self-effacing assistance, for to assist man is to serve his Creator—something worthy of only His attention.

Emphasized in Musar, all this is true of Judaism generally.

Musar's uniqueness is more basic.

Musar's uniqueness is the unification of "between man and G-d" and "between man and man" through *bein adam le'atzmo*, "between man and himself."

Bein adam le'atzmo is to work on oneself: to purify motives, to perfect integrity, to serve man and G-d without hypocrisy—to perform *mitzvos* because, and only because, Hashem commanded them.

In everything Rabbi Yosef Zundel did, he worked on himself. He consciously, carefully tried to make himself do as he said and say as he did.

He worked on himself when he made light of his piety.

He worked on himself when he dismissed compliments.

He did not deny self-worth. He affirmed humanity's highest worth: the capacity to acknowledge the greatness of Hashem. He demonstrated that a person could overcome the "normal" human receptivity to praise from out of sacred awareness of the paltriness of human praise. He demonstrated the capacity to do His will, to earn *His* praise.

In delivering a letter without warming to praise about himself, in helping a peddler without telling anyone about it, Rabbi Yosef Zundel acted from undiluted awareness that Hashem commanded him to be helpful and to be humble. He made personal integrity—"between man and himself"—the basis of both his "between man and G-d" and his "between man and man."

An additional point in Rabbi Yosef Zundel's piety, obvious yet easy to overlook: Rabbi Yosef Zundel *took time* to concentrate on piety. He not only freed his mind, he freed his schedule. He made time to work on himself.

One way he did this was to work on *bitachon*. He trusted that

Hashem would provide, also sensibly knowing that if his trust were defective, he temporarily had to return to work.

Even when he worked, it was to provide basics, not luxuries. Of course, he did not deny himself essentials, nor did he damage his health.

But neither did he pamper himself.

This made it easier to lay down the burdens of livelihood—to return to *bitachon*, to strengthen it. His freedom from working for a living freed time for work on Torah and Musar.

Said Rabbi Itzele Peterburger:

"People related awesome, wondrous incidents about Rabbi Yosef Zundel's *bitachon*." As if to emphasize the link between *bitachon* and the time it freed for pious acts, Rabbi Itzele continued: "And similarly, people used to relate Rabbi Yosef Zundel's great and wondrous acts—the steadfastness of his exactitude in performing *mitzvos*, and the power of his piety."

Bitachon seemed to be central in Rabbi Yosef Zundel's instruction to Reb Yisrael, for Reb Yisrael addressed *bitachon* in his earliest writings and communicated its importance to his disciples (the founder of Novorodock Musar was particularly responsive). Most indicative, Reb Yisrael worked on *bitachon* all his life. His aspiration to feel truly dependent on Hashem, truly sustained by Him—Him alone—was central.

Reb Yisrael offered food to a guest in his home.

"Here, you can eat this; for you, there is no doubt as to its *kashrus* [fitness]."

The guest was astounded. Could there be any doubt about the *kashrus* in the home of a preeminent Talmudic scholar and *tzaddik*? Further, could food even theoretically be kosher for one person, not for another?

Reb Yisrael explained:

"Unfortunately, I have recently had to accept support from wealthy laymen. If I do not accomplish what they expect of me, their support is stolen money in my hands. [The food I buy with this money might therefore be unfit, lacking ethical *kashrus*.] But with a transfer of possession (*shinui reshus*), stolen money loses it status as such. For you, there is not even a doubt about the *kashrus* of my food. Eat."

Reb Yisrael was distraught when his sense of dependence on Hashem decreased; he was exacting in handling other people's money. He joined two foci—"between man and G-d" and "between man and man"—in his effort to correlate both with personal honesty, with "between man and himself." To Reb Yisrael, holiness unified the spiritual, ethical, and psychological.

R abbi Yosef Zundel did nothing intentional to attract young Reb Yisrael. Reb Yisrael had to seek him out.

He could not know that Rabbi Yosef Zundel had a plan to help a forlorn peddler push a wagon up a hill.

He had to discover that.

He had to follow Rabbi Yosef Zundel, to make an effort to be in the unexpected places he sensed would witness Rabbi Yosef Zundel's piety.

And so, Reb Yisrael tracked Rabbi Yosef Zundel. He followed him into fields, for example. There, Rabbi Yosef Zundel studied Musar out loud. He formulated goals in helping others and in purifying intentions. A fire burned in Rabbi Yosef Zundel—an expressiveness, a spiritual power—to be revealed only in two ways: fully, for Hashem; selectively, for humanity. In the right disciple, Rabbi Yosef Zundel could kindle a burning desire to serve Hashem. He could sustain the right Jew in love of Hashem and His people all his life.

Reb Yisrael was the right Jew.

In observing Rabbi Yosef Zundel one day, Reb Yisrael slipped on a twig, or some such. He attracted Rabbi Zundel's attention. There followed one of the great moments in Jewish spiritual history.

Here was a young boy, secretly observing his ideal. Here was a ripened scholar and pietist, discovering he was being followed. The scholar had to respond to the moment—to a boy's yearning, to an opportunity to turn a moment of embarrassment into a lesson of the spirit.

Rabbi Yosef Zundel rose to the occasion, for his humility before Hashem included certainty about the way to it. He turned to the fledgling disciple, read the question on his face, told him how to proceed:

"Yisrael! Study Musar, that you may become one who fears Heaven!"

Simple words.

They transformed Reb Yisrael. They entered his heart "as a flaming arrow" (as he later put it). They constituted the prescription for the spiritual ascent to which he aspired, the ascent he had witnessed in Rabbi Yosef Zundel.

In Musar, simple words convey much. Words themselves are not the message. They are a code, a reference to a face of Torah apprehended by witnessing others live it, by living it oneself. In effect, Rabbi Yosef Zundel told Reb Yisrael: *"If you wish to understand and live Torah as I do, then study Musar books, which tell you how to work on yourself."*

Here was a sophisticated version of Hillel the Elder's message to the proselyte, "go study." The proselyte was told to study the commandments of Torah. Reb Yisrael already knew them. He was told to learn how to extract their deepest spiritual and ethical meaning.

Rabbi Yosef Zundel did not say, "go study in a library." He said: *"Musar is a treasure of spirit and deed. Although you, Yisrael, have only begun to acquire it, your intuition about your capacity to acquire it is correct. Go learn its lessons, go work on yourself to embody them."*

Reb Yisrael began to study Musar books, to intensify his prayer, to work on *bitachon,* to understand Talmudic study more profoundly—to perceive Hashem's requirements for piety and ethics.

As long as Rabbi Yosef Zundel remained in Salant, Reb Yisrael had a model against whom to measure himself, in consultation with whom he could improve himself. The best testimony to the altruism with which both Torah mentor (*rebbi*) and disciple imbued their task is mute testimony: the absence of information about them. For them, the task itself was the thing, not talking or writing about it. From Reb Yisrael's arrival in Salant in about 1822 until both his and Rabbi Yosef Zundel's departure in 1838, we know next to nothing about them, save their decisive meeting and subsequent relationship.

We know that Reb Yisrael married young, as was the custom; we know two incidents. The first, about Reb Yisrael's marriage, shows the Musar heritage he received from his parents. The second, about him and his wife, shows how he internalized his heritage.

Reb Yisrael's parents arranged his engagement to Esther Feige, daughter of Rabbi and Mrs. Yaakov Eisenstein of Salant, descendents of the holy *Sh'lah*. The Eisensteins promised a dowry of 300 rubles.

Later, their finances deteriorated. The 300 rubles were no longer available. Word of developments reached a well-to-do individual, who offered the Eisensteins 10,000 rubles to withdraw their daughter in favor of his own. Since the Eisensteins could not keep their part of the bargain, Rabbi Eisenstein traveled to Reb Yisrael's parents in Zagory to suggest they cancel with him, and instead take 10,000 rubles for a new match.

Reb Yisrael's father paid no attention to all this. He called his wife. All three drank *lechayyim* and fixed the date for the wedding.

The one side—the Eisensteins—had struck a deal they could not keep, so they offered to withdraw, notwithstanding the loss of a unique scholar to the family. The other side—the Lipkins—had every right to withdraw, but they wished to consider feelings, lineage (*yichus*), and *lifnim mishuras hadin*, "going beyond the letter of the law"; notwithstanding the monetary loss in rejecting the Eisensteins' offer to cancel. And so, Reb Yisrael married Esther Feige Eisenstein.

The newlyweds agreed to divide responsibilities: Reb Yisrael would handle all "heavenly matters," Esther Feige all "worldly matters." Throughout their lives, however, they could not identify a single matter as purely secular, or "worldly." Everything was linked by law (halachah), or by "going beyond the law," to "Heaven."

When Rabbi Yosef Zundel ascended to Jerusalem in 1838, intense self-examination overcame Reb Yisrael. Should he continue in the path of hidden piety of his *rebbi*? There was an advantage. He could avoid the spiritually contaminating influence of public praise for his knowledge and sensitivity. Reb Yisrael concluded, however, that there was a public role for which he was uniquely suited. To shirk this role would be to disregard his destiny.

Reb Yisrael noticed weaknesses in the fabric of Lithuanian Jewry. He noticed that *Haskalah* ("Enlightenment") was growing, that traditional society was vulnerable.

Given Reb Yisrael's perceptions (proven correct), he conceived his purpose differently from Rabbi Yosef Zundel. His own task was to set forth Musar as an antidote to *Haskalah*. In Reb Yisrael's hands, Musar became more than a refined level of Jewish living.

It became a tool of Jewish survival.

With the emergence of alternatives to Talmud study and halachic observance, Lithuanian Jewry would remain faithful only through the cultivation of joy and awe in study and observance. Cultivation required extra effort, and that would require a framework—a Musar movement. Therefore, Reb Yisrael set out to secure a respected position from which to launch a Musar movement.

Through his first public lectures in Talmud, his name spread far and wide. He was invited to lecture in Talmud in Vilna, "the Jerusalem of Lithuania." He achieved his immediate goal, a respected position. He also faced temptations. In disseminating Torah and Musar, Reb Yisrael now had to cope with the posturing and publicity that a public role could foster.

He met the challenge in three ways.

First: He remained constantly conscious of the challenge. He had no illusion that public service either exempted him from Musar tasks of humility and honesty or guaranteed success at meeting them.

He knew the necessity and had the ability to step outside himself, to engage in self-analysis, to look at himself as others did. He could know when public duties threatened to corrupt his *avodas Hashem*.

Second: He scheduled regular periods of withdrawal from public life. He retired to a *bes hisbodedus*, a private Musar room, to pour out his soul to Hashem. In the aftermath of a spiritually trying episode, he could analyze what had gone wrong, and what right. Scheduling periodic withdrawal from the public arena, he could keep in touch with himself and his goals.

Third: Temptation in *zikkui harabbim* (public service, or "turning the many to righteousness") was obvious. Was there an advantage? Reb Yisrael concluded there was. "*He who turns the many to righteousness is never an instrument for sin*," says the Talmud (*Yoma* 87b). Reb Yisrael explored the psychological dynamics—the Musar possibilities—of this promise.

Public service, he discovered, helps prevent self-absorption—an occupational hazard of Musar. Self-analysis can foster the opposite of its intended goal; search for humility and honesty can lead to exclusive self-concern. Public service, on the other hand, shifts attention from oneself to others. It guards against unhealthy preoccupation with oneself. Public service is a handmaiden of Musar, suppressing and ultimately sublimating self-centeredness.

What is more, interaction with people reveals aspects of personality not revealed privately, in Musar rooms. Just as introspection nurtures the capacity to step outside oneself, to see oneself, so does cooperation in work on public projects.

In Vilna, Reb Yisrael set out to "turn the many to righteousness." He rooted his efforts in Torah study. On first arriving in Vilna, he assumed his post in Talmud in Ramailles yeshiva.[1] From then until he left Vilna in 1849, he taught Talmud regularly and intensively, first in Ramailles, then across the river in the Vilna suburb of Zariche.

---

1. Ramailles yeshiva flourished until 1939. After World War II, Rabbi Yisrael Gustman reestablished it, successively, in New York and Jerusalem.

Talmud study, though indispensable, was insufficient to launch a Musar movement. Talmud study did not reach the whole community; it could not even sustain all of its students, given the challenge of *Haskalah.*

To reach the whole community, Reb Yisrael innovated:

• He delivered public lectures on fear of Heaven to lay people—something new for first-rank yeshiva deans. He taught females as well as males—also something new. And essential. To quote Reb Yisrael (*Or Yisrael*, letter #3):

> Musar study is unlike all other Jewish studies. There is no other study as comprehensively obligatory. . . . Women are exempt from *Talmud Torah* [Torah study]; there is also much room to exempt those truly suffering for lack of livelihood or truly limited in mental capacity—each according to his situation is correspondingly removed from the obligation of *Talmud Torah*. . . . This is not the case with Musar study. It is obligatory for everyone. No one is exempt, since the war against unworthy desires embraces every speaking being.

• Reb Yisrael tailored his lectures to the learned and unlearned alike, since in his view the learned, too, were vulnerable to *Haskalah.* In attracting different strata to his public sermons, he helped heal divisions in Vilna Jewry.

• He opened *batei Musar*, special Musar rooms. Talmud was studied in a yeshiva or synagogue, while *batei Musar* were for different purposes: introspection; recitation of Musar books; analysis of personality and piety; and other techniques of *bein adam le'atzmo*, of discovering and repairing roots of sin and defects of character.

Reb Yisrael and his disciples studied Musar books as repositories of Torah ethics—as objective information—but also as springboards to self-scrutiny. In the Musar room, resistance could be great, results painful. To weaken resistance, *ba'alei Musar* did not just read Musar books. Musar study was not passive. It was active: reciting, humming, singing, sometimes even shouting—studying with "lips aflame." It was the search for moving Scriptural verses, and their repeated recitation—the clearing of the mind of everything but the idea that a given verse articulated. It was a discipline in concentrating the mind, in looking clearly, steadily, starkly into one's soul.

Self-knowledge, derived *personally,* was acquired mostly inside *batei Musar;* derived *interpersonally,* mostly outside *batei Musar*—but in relation to them.

In persuading others to undertake Musar study, *ba'alei Musar* came to know themselves. As Musar outreach became fine-tuned, as active Musar rooms emerged, the human interaction illuminated sides of self inaccessible through private concentration on the soul. In Musar rooms, and in persuading others to come to them, *ba'alei Musar* witnessed their behavior in every circumstance. They saw what they needed to analyze. They identified biases and character defects—their psychological makeup.

Reb Yisrael would be called the precursor of contemporary outreach were it not that he himself founded the first outreach programs in Germany, years after he left Lithuania. For German Jews, whose belief and observance were essentially in decline, Reb Yisrael adapted techniques he used with Lithuanian Jews, whose belief and observance were essentially intact.

Reb Yisrael is the founder of both reaching-out and reaching-in, of extending a hand to potential returnees or *ba'alei teshuvah,* and of strengthening Torah Jewry.

The result of Reb Yisrael's work on himself and his communities—his efforts to harness Musar teachings in his own life and times—was the remarkable sensitivity for which his very name has become a symbol.

&§ Reb Yisrael was crossing the river from Vilna to Zaritche, where he delivered his Talmudic lectures. He noticed a distraught woman below the bridge, near the river. He scurried down to stop her from throwing herself into the river—from committing suicide. Knowing the Talmudic passage which calls a man who sees a drowning woman, but refuses to save her for reasons of modesty, a "pious idiot," Reb Yisrael bodily restrained the young woman. He then coaxed her to talk.

She said she had lost two children, whereupon her husband fell into depression. This all but eliminated their livelihood. She collected only a small rental for her husband's horse and carriage, as he could no longer drive.

That day, the horse died.

She had no reason to live: no children, no husband (to speak of), no livelihood.

Reb Yisrael spoke at length. He soothed and strengthened her. She was still young, he said. She could still bear children. Her husband could recover.

Then, in a gesture typical of Reb Yisrael's belief that fine intentions and rhetoric were insufficient, he told her that he would send the funds to buy a new horse.

And he did.

A year later, he received an invitation to a *bris milah*, a circumcision.

ৎৡ In Memel, Reb Yisrael confronted double anguish on the *yahrzeit* (anniversary of death) of his father. Jewish law rules that when two or more people observe *yahrzeit* the same day, the ritual obligations fall first on one who observes his father's *yahrzeit*. In addition, Reb Yisrael ruled in accord with the halachic position that only one person should recite *kaddish* at one time.

That day, a man observed his daughter's *yahrzeit*.

The obligation to recite *kaddish* was Reb Yisrael's.

Noticing, however, that the man who had lost his daughter was acutely distressed at the prospect of not reciting *kaddish*, Reb Yisrael told him to do so.

Many congregants expressed surprise at Reb Yisrael's decision, as he ostensibly had no right to make light of his father's honor.

Reb Yisrael replied that the merit of *gemillus chasadim*—alleviating distress—was greater than the merit of *kaddish*.

ৠ Reb Yisrael was approached by a poor, broken man. He could eke out a living only by passing from town to town, delivering a homily (*derashah*), then passing the hat. But he knew no homiletic material. Would Reb Yisrael teach him? Moved by the man's plight, Reb Yisrael—internationally renowned scholar— taught the prospective preacher a fine homily, then practiced it with him until he had it down.

ৠ According to a statement Reb Yisrael made to Reb Itzele Peterburger, Reb Yisrael never ceased to think in Torah or Musar for longer than it takes to walk six feet (*daled amos*). Fear of Heaven pervaded his consciousness. Yet one day in Vilna he traded in idle conversation with a Jew in the street. Even more: Reb Yisrael told jokes, tried to make the Jew laugh.

It appeared out of character.

One of Reb Yisrael's disciples worked up the courage to question the *rebbi's* deviation. Reb Yisrael responded that this Jew was depressed, embittered. There was no better response than to take the sting out of his sadness.

ৠ Reb Yisrael went to great lengths to secure Passover *matzah* whose *kashrus* fulfilled even optional criteria. His students once requested last minute instructions in setting out for the *matzah* bakery, expecting to hear a review of *kashrus* requirements. Instead, they heard Reb Yisrael caution them not to overwork the women preparing the dough, not to insist that they work so quickly as to damage their health, even though speed is at the heart of preparing kosher-for-Passover *matzah*.

ৠ Kovno and Slobodka were twin towns, separated only by a small river. Once, a woman died without money to pay for her funeral. The burial societies of Kovno and Slobodka took to disputing which one was responsible for her care prior to burial, and for the burial itself.

The argument took place in the synagogue during *shema*, which requires special concentration.

It is a major desecration to leave a dead body unattended,

to delay ritual purification (washing of the body) and other funeral preparations. The obligation to bury a *mes mitzvah*—a person with no one to attend to his or her interment—falls on any Jew in the vicinity at the time of death.

Reb Yisrael, overhearing the arguing of the burial societies, found it an intolerable provocation of the requirement not to desecrate a corpse—not to delay burial. He ruled that the woman was a *mes mitzvah*, considered himself responsible for her burial, interrupted his recitation of *shema*, removed his *tefilin*, and instructed his disciples to do the same. They buried the woman.

In the summer of 1848, cholera struck Vilna. Medical knowledge and public health were insufficient to prevent mass death. Reb Yisrael voluntarily established a makeshift hospital, secured the services of physicians, and organized platoons of yeshiva students to care for the ill.

He issued lenient halachic rulings about cooking on Sabbath, since hot food could make the difference between life and death.[1]

As Yom Kippur approached, Reb Yisrael worried about the consequences of fasting and intensive praying.

They could bring death.

Versions differ as to what Reb Yisrael did on that Yom Kippur.

Most versions agree that he ruled it obligatory to eat, to shorten services, to take walks in the fresh air, and that he himself publicly recited *kiddush* (the blessing over sacramental wine). He prohibited normal Yom Kippur observance to save lives.

Reb Yisrael's rulings aroused much controversy, especially since he never before issued halachic decisions.

To respond to the controversy, Reb Yisrael delivered a Talmudic lecture. His critics expected him to defend himself. Instead, he brilliantly addressed other topics. He marshalled more sources and revealed his Talmudic acumen more extensively than ever before.

---

1. The saving of human life takes precedent over every *mitzvah*, save three. One cannot commit murder, idolatry, or adultery to save a life, including one's own. It is necessary to consult pertinent halachic sources for the precise circumstances in which the surpassing obligation to save a life applies, and in which the exceptions apply.

Critics were silenced.

A scholar of this stature could not err.

The controversy over Reb Yisrael's rulings during the cholera epidemic set in motion a short-range defeat and long-range victory for the Musar movement.

The controversy, and Reb Yisrael's emphasis on ethics and renewal, called his attention to *maskilim* (early intellectual "enlighteners"). This triggered the Musar movement's short-range defeat.

In Lithuania, *Haskalah* ("Enlightenment") passed through stages, the early ones being the most destructive of Jewish interests. From 1825 to 1855, Tsar Nicholas I enforced "Cantonist decrees," under which Jewish boys were taken from their homes at the age of 12 for 31 years, including 25 years of military service and forced conversion to Russian Orthodox Christianity. Despite evasions by Jewish parents, 50,000 young Jews were lost to Judaism and the Jewish community—one of the tragedies of the Exile.

But some *maskilim* made common cause with anti-Semitic Tsar Nicholas I and his minions, who wished to dilute yeshiva education. Ostensibly, yeshiva students were to be introduced to Russian language and other secular studies. In fact, curricular reform was a front. Yeshiva students were to assimilate or apostasize. They were to be "Russified"—turned into unobservant, Russian intellectuals—or actually put through a formal conversion to Russian Christianity.

The transformation was to occur through Tsarist-sponsored schools for Jewish children. The organizers were Count Sergei Uvarov, the Tsar's Minister of Education, *maskilim*, and Max Lilienthal, a young German Reform Jew who later conceded he had been duped.

The flagship Tsarist school was to be a new rabbinical seminary in Vilna. Count Uvarov, upon counsel of *maskilim*, offered the deanship of the seminary to Reb Yisrael.

Reb Yisrael had never supported Vilna's *maskilim*, but the mere fact they offered him this position tainted him, he thought. It was not enough to refuse the position. He had to dissociate himself radically from Vilna's Tsarist collaborators. He had to leave Vilna altogether.

His departure was the short-range defeat for the Musar movement. His direct nurture in Vilna of Musar rooms, and of ba'alei Musar and Talmud scholars (often they were the same people), ceased.

The long-range victory for the Musar movement was Reb Yisrael's follow-up on the lesson he learned from his trouble with maskilim. The lesson was clear: danger in Haskalah was not a long way off, as he had thought; it was now. The follow-up was clear: reversal of tactics. Reb Yisrael stopped working as if he alone could disseminate Musar among Lithuanian Jewry. He turned his energies from the community-at-large to select disciples who, he hoped, would coalesce as the leadership of a movement that would surpass him.

Arriving in Kovno in 1849, Reb Yisrael founded a small yeshiva. He concentrated on training Talmudic prodigies who would spearhead the Musar movement, ensure its vitality for generations to come. Reb Yisrael's major disciples included Rabbis Simcha Zisl Ziv (the Alter of Kelm), Itzele Peterburger, and Naftali Amsterdam.

Reb Yisrael molded them in accord with such Musar concepts as integrity ("between man and himself"), helpfulness ("between man and man"), and bitachon ("between man and G-d"). He taught them how comprehensive study of Torah—study with the Musar lens—brought these concepts into sharp, and practical, focus.

Comprehensive study of Torah gave vague feelings associated with human relations or spiritual aspirations precise definition.

Example:

When the holy sage of the pre-World War II generation, the Chafetz Chaim, completed his innovative book on slander and talebearing, he submitted it to Reb Yisrael (who, according to some traditions, inspired the Chafetz Chaim to pursue this kind of scholarship).

Reb Yisrael was deeply moved by the work. It brought to

completion the kind of aspiration he nurtured throughout his career. It classified and codified halachic requirements for ethical conduct, giving new power and respect to the topic of proper speech.

It brought the Musar face of Torah to perfect crystallization.

Or almost perfect.

Reb Yisrael objected to one formulation of the Chafetz Chaim.

If a person offends someone without his knowledge (a person defames Reuben's name in the presence of Simeon, but the defamation never reaches Reuben's ears), what is the remedy? The Chafetz Chaim wrote that the offender must seek pardon from Reuben for defaming him. The offender must seek pardon no later than the eve of Yom Kippur, in accord with the requirement to enter the holy day of judgment with a clean slate in human dealings.

Wrong, said Reb Yisrael.

The requirement to clean one's slate cannot be fulfilled at another person's expense. Because Reuben does not know he has been defamed, the offender's seeking pardon from Reuben can only bring Reuben anguish—for the first time he learns his name has been blackened. One has no right to a clean slate on Yom Kippur if this is accomplished by causing anguish. The offender must do penance by building up Reuben's reputation.

The Chafetz Chaim replied that he based his ruling on Rabbenu Yonah, the authoritative medieval scholar (rishon).

Reb Yisrael remained unmoved.

Almost a century later, the question was put to Rabbi Aharon Kotler, preeminent Lakewood yeshiva dean: "Who was right, Reb Yisrael or the Chafetz Chaim?"

Rabbi Kotler thought a moment, then replied:

"Reb Yisrael, tanna hu u-palig"—Reb Yisrael is like a Talmudic sage whose scholarship was so impeccable and whose personal stature so close to an earlier generation's, that he had the right to disagree with a sage (tanna) of the earlier, more authoritative Mishnaic epoch. With respect to the face of Torah called Musar, the scholarship of Reb Yisrael was so impeccable and his personal stature so close to earlier generations', that he had the right to disagree with Rabbenu Yonah, a sage of the earlier, more authoritative medieval epoch.

Reb Yisrael was so impressive that *gedolei yisrael* who emerged from the Musar movement regarded him as a throwback to an earlier period, much as Rabbi Zvi Broide termed young Reb Yisrael "an *Alfasi katan*."

Three generations after Reb Yisrael lived and taught, *gedolei yisrael* were still warming themselves by his spiritual light, first prepared for posterity when he came to Kovno in 1849.

R eb Yisrael was ahead of his time. Even as his career brought new vitality to parts of Lithuanian Jewry, he knew this was not enough. This alone would not stop assimilation.

Reb Yisrael left Lithuania in about 1858 to undertake outreach projects, most of which failed in their own time, all of which are now taken for granted. Perhaps, Reb Yisrael felt a certain freedom to expand his efforts after he had laid a solid foundation for the Musar movement. Perhaps, he felt that Jewish spiritual welfare in Eastern Europe was tied to Western Europe—perhaps. We cannot be certain, since very few documents and oral traditions about Reb Yisrael's long sojourn in the West exist.

But one thing is certain.

Reb Yisrael's vision was broad, his goals were comprehensive.

He wished to see a return to full observance by all Jews turning away from Torah study and *mitzvos*.

Reb Yisrael originally left Kovno for medical treatment in Prussia. The question, then, is not why he left Lithuania, but why he stayed in Western Europe. He did return to Lithuania, once (perhaps twice) for two years; he did remain in contact with disciples. But most of this period—1858 to 1883—he lived in Prussia and Paris.

There is only one oral tradition attributed to Reb Yisrael on his drastic move, the first of its kind by a preeminent East European Torah scholar, a *gadol beyisrael*. Said Reb Yisrael:

> When horses panic on a mountaintop and begin to gallop downhill, they cannot be restrained. Whoever tries to halt them will endanger his life; the horses will surely trample him. Once the horses have reached level ground,

however, it is possible to bridle them, to bring them under control.

So it is with rejuvenation of Judaism.

In Russia, the large Jewish communities gallop on a downward spiritual slope; it is impossible to bring them to order. But the German communities have been on level ground for some time; it is possible to halt them, to restore them.

Reb Yisrael perceived limits, even dangers, in trying to fortify a deteriorating religious community, while a religious community already defeated could be rebuilt.

Reb Yisrael spent many years in such German cities as Berlin, Memel, Halberstadt, Friedrichstadt, and Koenigsberg, trying to win back laymen and college students to Torah Judaism. He proposed several innovative projects to revitalize German Jewish communities weakened by Reform, assimilation, and apostasy. He could not bring these projects to fruition; he was ahead of his time.

The projects included:

• preparation of an Aramaic-Hebrew dictionary to facilitate study of Talmud;

• translation of the Talmud from Aramaic to make it accessible to beginners;

• elucidation of methodological principles of Talmud study;

• introduction of Talmud into college curricula to establish respect for it among Gentiles—this, as a way to establish respect for Talmud among Jewish students who would not respect it in its own right;

• publication, in Russian, of Jewish books for assimilating Russian Jews.

The first Torah journal, *Tevunah*, was the only one of Reb Yisrael's German-period projects which met with some success. Published from 1861 to 1862, it contained some of Reb Yisrael's advanced thinking on psychology and Torah.

Reb Yisrael's articles in *Tevunah* indicate that he was ahead of his time not just in innovative ideas for outreach, but in ideas per se. Still more: Reb Yisrael linked intellectual to communal innovation.

To Reb Yisrael, life was not to be a series of compartmentalized endeavors, in which ideas were separate from action, intellectual perspectives separate from communal ones. Life was to reflect the Musar ideal of harmony or *shelemus*, the blending of life's endeavors, personal and communal; and, within the personal, the blending of psychological health, halachic observance, and piety.

Reb Yisrael tied intellectual to communal innovation by defining Jewish communal leadership as *da'as Torah*. To the best of my knowledge, Reb Yisrael was the first to use *"da'as Torah"* ("the Torah perspective") to connote a preeminent Talmudic scholar's application of his knowledge to personal and communal issues.

Reb Yisrael regarded his perspective as "the Torah perspective." Accordingly, he involved himself in communal issues.

• He convened or attended meetings of rabbinic leadership to plot strategy to alter anti-Semitic, Tsarist decrees; or, in one instance, such a meeting was cancelled at his behest because he deemed it unwise.

• He arranged for a Jewish lobbyist to live and work in St. Petersburg for 28 years to prevent anti-Semitic decrees.

• He himself traveled to St. Petersburg to lobby Tsarist authorities.

What is the basis of communal leadership of *da'as Torah*?

Here we reach Reb Yisrael's intellectual innovation.

To Reb Yisrael, spiritual decline in the generations has rendered Jews imperfect receptacles of Torah. Torah study alone—teaching the intellect Torah—does not sufficiently sanctify a person. There remain evil urges and biases which distort not only personal sanctity, but intellect.

To purify intellect—to make it an unbiased receptacle of Torah—Musar work (*bein adam le'atzmo*) is necessary. Musar work suppresses and sublimates distorting urges and biases. Musar work nurtures serenity and clarity—*shelemus*.

Shelemus is more than psychologically satisfying; it is essential to Torah study and observance. On the purest level, *shelemus* turns the intellectually talented Talmud scholar into more than a scholar. He becomes the bearer of *da'as Torah*. He becomes harmonious and unbiased, capable of seeing clearly, steadily, and starkly into his own soul, the soul of others, the soul of the Jewish nation.

This is the bearer of *da'as Torah*.

This was Reb Yisrael.

The foundation of Reb Yisrael's ideas was a new formulation of freedom of choice (later elaborated by his great-grandson, Rabbi Eliyahu Eliezer Dessler, in *Michtav Me-Eliyahu*).

Reb Yisrael's new formulation is necessitated by the Jew's new condition, by the decline in the generations. Not only evil urges and biases, but *unconscious* urges and biases rule the Jew. In order to change them, a Jew must first know them. Musar study, in concentrating the mind, and Musar outreach, in intensifying human interaction, slowly bring deeper levels of consciousness up for conscious examination. Even so, unconscious biases and urges overpower the capacity for conscious decision; a person does not act freely most of the time.

His unconscious rules him.

This is true—continued Reb Yisrael—but Musar methods do more than reveal the unconscious. They slowly change it. Musar work is difficult and complex. It can take years to change one unworthy trait, but it can be done.

And it was done.

By Reb Yisrael himself and by his major disciples.

The foundation of their achievement was freedom of choice.

A person, said Reb Yisrael, cannot wish or "will" away an unworthy urge or bias. He can choose to (or not to) undertake the Musar methods which eventually correct it. Faced with a *mitzvah* of Torah and propelled by a contrary urge or bias (conscious or unconscious), a Jew can work on himself to follow the Torah. He can gradually reduce the strength of his unworthy urge or bias, and increase his will to perform *mitzvos*.

With dedicated effort, he crosses two lines. The first line is performance. The Jew sufficiently reduces his anti-Torah urge to perform a *mitzvah*.

He changes behavior.

But he is left with mixed motives; he is still drawn to an unworthy urge or bias, even without acting on it. He then crosses the second line, purifying his motives. Even if wholly observant, a Jew can and must purify motives.

A Jew's capacity to choose in favor of Torah (or the opposite) never leaves him unless he works on himself so thoroughly that he comes to perform a *mitzvah* purely, with no evil urge or bias remaining, even unconsciously. On this sublime level, the Jew is no longer free to choose against Torah. Ironically, the ultimate goal of freedom of choice is to eliminate it, to perform every *mitzvah* naturally and wholly.

This is the level of the preeminent Talmudic scholar.

This is the bearer of *da'as Torah*—the *adam hashalem*, the harmonious man of Torah.

W̱hat was the relation between Reb Yisrael's prescription for West European Jewry and the program of German Orthodoxy's leader, Rabbi Shimshon Refael Hirsch?

Reb Yisrael viewed favorably Rabbi Hirsch's *Torah im derech eretz* ("Torah and general culture"). He also esteemed Rabbi Hirsch's colleague, Rabbi Ezriel Hildesheimer. However, what Reb Yisrael approved in Germany, he approved for Germany. He believed that intensive, exclusive study of Torah and Musar generated a level of purity that could not be duplicated by the Hirschian curriculum for transforming secular studies in light of Torah.

At the same time, Rabbi Yisrael's Musar emphasis on introspection and integrity legitimized the need for a Jew, already exposed to secular studies, to refashion his secular interests in light of Torah. To be both honest and psychologically healthy, such a Jew, under the discipline of Musar, had to acknowledge his inclinations, as he sought to mold them in accord with Torah.

Some of Reb Yisrael's disciples, particularly in Novorodock Musar (Chapter 8), emphasized purity, arising from exclusive study of Torah and Musar. Other disciples, particularly in Kelm Musar (Chapter 5), and like the Hirschian program, addressed philosophical issues. The emotional and introspective inflection of all Musar schools distinguished them from *Torah im derech eretz*.

Reb Yisrael's chief disciple (*talmid muvhak*), the Alter of Kelm, illuminated both the difference in tone between Musar and the Hirschian approach, and the difficulty in tracing Reb Yisrael's steps in Western Europe.

> Let none of those who knew Reb Yisrael in his last years think that they really knew him. . . . The truth is that even in his younger years Reb Yisrael's conception of holiness included extreme self-concealment. My knowledge on this point is completely certain. Even when Reb Yisrael was active in public matters he never revealed more than that which the occasion required, whether in Torah or piety. However . . . whoever knew Reb Yisrael at the end of his days knew him not at all, regardless of what he might imagine. We who knew Reb Yisrael from earlier years, when he was publicly active, knew that we could know him . . . only through an exacting process of clarification. Similarly, we would hear a statement from him, interpret it in our own way, and then, several years later, it became known to us from him that a different point inhered in the statement—a point that would occur to virtually no one. This happened countless times . . . Even with my scanty knowledge of Reb Yisrael, several long pages would not suffice to recount a few of his wondrous ways. My intention here is simply to inform those who knew him at the end of his days that they can easily deceive themselves into believing that they knew him, and thus fall into the category of those who don't know that they don't know.

Any true *tzaddik*, such as Reb Yisrael, is ultimately a mystery. In apprehending a *tzaddik*, we must acknowledge the limitation of words.

On Reb Yisrael and his disciples, we can say much before reaching the ultimate barrier. We turn, now, to Reb Yisrael's disciples—to the Musar movement itself—but just one last incident, the story of Reb Yisrael's death, in Koenigsberg, 25 Shevat, 5643 (1883):

The Jewish community in Koenigsberg assigned a watchman to stay with Reb Yisrael. A *gadol beyisrael* who is ill and alone—away from family and disciples—should not be left unattended. On the night that Reb Yisrael sensed was his last, the watchman was frightened, afraid to be alone in a room with a dead body. A teacher of introspection and repentance, Reb Yisrael, we may imagine, would have liked to spend his last moments reviewing his life and repenting. Perhaps this is what he did, inwardly. Outwardly, he practiced what he preached: personal spiritual burdens should not take precedence over the needs of another human being. And so, Reb Yisrael talked with the watchman, tried to soothe him. He tried to ease his fears, to convince him that there was no danger in remaining alone with a corpse—his own.

Part Three: The Musar Movement's First-Generation Disciples

5.

Kelm Musar

ake time. Be exact. Unclutter the mind . . .

For years I resisted an investigation of "Kelm," the Musar of Reb Yisrael's preeminent disciple, Rabbi Simcha Zisl Ziv, "the Alter of Kelm."

I resisted.

And more.

I fell prey to the trait that Musar says lies at the heart of divergence from truth: rationalization. Since I was not privileged to know Kelm disciples personally, how could I understand their *derech* or orientation?

I fell prey further, to a secondary snare, raising rationalization to a higher plane, endowing self-deception with righteousness:

Without personal knowledge of Kelm, how could I do it justice, meet high standards?

Modesty and high standards: *rationalization*.

The truth is that Kelm could be the most relevant of all Musar schools in the present age. High-minded justification for not confronting the teachings of Kelm amount to a fear that here is Musar quite direct and pertinent, and, in consequence, perhaps more obligatory than joyous Novorodock or lofty Slobodka Musar.

At least for me.

Perhaps I had avoided Kelm because it is what I needed most.

Perhaps I had avoided it because it speaks to impatience and spiritual uncertainty, to conditions that reflect lack of discipline or self-confidence. *Take time*, said the Alter of Kelm. Be confident that a relationship with man, with Hashem, and with the Torah can work itself into your life. *Be exact*, he said, for it is easier to pursue perfection than ultimately unsatisfying short-cuts. *Unclutter the mind*, he said. Learn to guide your *sechel* or reasoning and there will be no limit to the confidence and clarity, the achievement and tranquillity, you can generate.

As coming chapters will show, Novorodock Musar requires a unique capacity for self-transcendence, Slobodka Musar requires a special sensitivity of soul. Kelm Musar is more cautious—less exuberant—than either Novorodock or Slobodka. And, not to be forgotten, Kelm is the motherlode of Musar, the rich vein whence Novorodock and Slobodka sprang. Kelm is the closest to the source: the teachings of Reb Yisrael Salanter himself. If for this reason alone, it deserves scrutiny.

An unmistakable tonality animated the teachings and the life of the Alter of Kelm and of his great disciples. These remarkable masters of Torah, and of themselves, were calm and serious, tranquil and deliberate, alert to the needs of others, outgoing, helpful. The stress in Kelm on punctuality, neatness, and intellectual advancement step-by-step had its goal in expansiveness of mind and soul. If everything were in place, physically, and everything done in its proper time, intellectually and spiritually, the disciple of Kelm had the time, desire, and ability to be at peace with himself, his neighbor, his world.

The Alter of Kelm worked relentlessly at teaching the need for order in living and thinking, with results wondrous to behold: All major Musar schools and personalities took their nurture, in whole or in part, from Kelm.

Directly from Kelm there emerged such deep thinkers as Reb Yisrael Salanter's great-grandson, Rabbi Eliyahu Eliezer Dessler (author of *Michtav Me-Eliyahu*), Rabbi Yerucham Levovitz of Mir (author of *Da'as Chochmah Umusar*), and Rabbi Moshe Rosenstein of Lomz (author of *Yesodei Hada'as*).

Indirectly from Kelm came the legendary Alter of Novorodock and Alter of Slobodka, fathers of their own Musar disciplines, doctrines, and disciples.

All disciples of the Alter of Kelm were traceable to his yeshivas— "Beis Hatalmud" and "Talmud Torah"—in which his special service of Hashem, and his special pedagogic ways of transmitting it, flourished.

◆§ There was no *shamash*, nor even a custodian or janitor, in Beis Hatalmud. All maintenance work was performed by the yeshiva students themselves. They considered this a privilege, and even vied for particular jobs when they were "auctioned" to bidders on Rosh Hashanah.

This system was central to the Alter's educational philosophy of molding the whole person, not just the mind. Through his system of student-run maintenance, the Alter nurtured total service of Torah. In doing so, he nurtured a variety of worthy traits, such as promptness, cooperation, and helpfulness. Self-control in externals—punctuality, neatness, cleanliness— would foster self-control in thought and action.

◆§ Once, a visitor to Beis Hatalmud forgot his cane. This same person visited Beis Hatalmud 13 years later, only to find the cane hanging from the very same peg on which he had left it.

◄§ When people crossed the entrance to Beis Hatalmud, they sometimes thought the building was absolutely empty, since it was absolutely silent. Upon further exploration, they saw the entire student body praying *Shemoneh Esrei*, the silent Eighteen Benedictions, standing straight, facing ahead, motionless, feet together, hands at sides, completely silent—yet praying with great intensity and concentration.

◄§ When Moshe Rosenstein first walked into Beis Hatalmud as a youth, a student approached him and extended greetings, asked when he had arrived, and showed him where to eat and sleep. The welcome was so heartfelt that for a moment young Rosenstein thought that here was an old friend whom he had forgotten. A moment later another student approached with the same greetings, the same help. The future *mashgiach* in Lomz wondered at his loss of memory for friends. Only when student after student similarly approached him did he realize that unusual consideration for newcomers was standard in Kelm.

All of the exemplary qualities which the Alter's disciples came to embody were embodied in the Alter himself. We know this for a simple reason: The Alter never demanded any spiritual or behavioral ideal from his disciples unless he first demanded it of himself, and mastered it himself.

The Alter's aversion to hypocrisy derived from his eight years of tutelage under Reb Yisrael Salanter—this, after he demonstrated great potential on his own.

The Alter's father, Rabbi Yisrael Broide, studied under Reb Yisrael's first *rebbi* (Rabbi Zvi Hirsh Broide) and even met Reb Yisrael in Salant. Rabbi Yisrael Broide knew the entire Talmud thoroughly, and many parts of it by heart.

The Alter's mother was both learned and pious—learned, in particular, in Talmudic laws of women, and so pious that even at the funeral of her only daughter, she did what she always did at funerals. She collected *tzedakah* for the poor.

Added to young Simcha Zisl's nurture in the atmosphere of parents such as these was his own talent and industry. Already by Bar Mitzvah he could compose a *hadran* or review of an entire Talmudic division, *Nezikin*. He married young, and was determined to continue his sacred studies.

At 25, when he learned of Reb Yisrael Salanter's new and unique study house in Kovno he traveled there, partly out of curiosity, partly to oppose Reb Yisrael's approach. Once there, however, he was won over completely. Reb Yisrael's penetrating Musar analysis, according to which an absolutely true understanding of Torah could not emerge from a mind plagued by rationalization and self-deception, penetrated Rabbi Simcha Zisl to the core.

He devoted a full year to nothing but the teachings and the practice of Musar.

He learned that when a person is biased or deficient in character, he cannot fully grasp Torah, no matter how intelligent or learned he is. Rabbi Simcha Zisl learned that a person had to subject both his presuppositions and his personality to theoretical analysis and concrete means of *tikkun*, or repair, in order to become a true student of Torah.

In studying Torah and Musar under Reb Yisrael, Rabbi Simcha Zisl brought two related talents to great development.

First: his *hasmadah* or assiduity in Talmud study. He adopted the discipline of the Vilna Gaon, who slept only two-and-a-half hours in every 24, and divided those two-and-a-half-hours into five one-half hour slots. In this framework, Rabbi Simcha Zisl studied 12 straight hours, following the evening prayers until the morning prayers, in the winter. In the summer, he prayed with sunrise (*vasikin*) and then sat in study straight through to 2:00 p.m.

With slight variation, he maintained this schedule until the last years of his life.

At his funeral, in 1898, a colleague from their days together under Reb Yisrael in Kovno, the renowned Telshe yeshiva dean Rabbi Eliezer Gordon, testified that the Alter of Kelm knew three *sedarim* or divisions of Talmud (including *Rashi* and *Tosafos*) by heart; and that he knew all four divisions of the *Shulchan Aruch*, including every single identifying number (*se'if katan*) of the thousands of comments by the major commentaries.

Second: his concentration. The Alter honed his ability to concentrate to such an extent that he could:

• simultaneously carry on a conversation and "think in Talmud learning";

• recall at the end of the day everything he had thought throughout the day (for the purpose of evaluating his thoughts);

• seal his mind hermetically from all distracting thoughts and events for hours at a time, in concentrating on his chosen topic;

• review a single chapter or section of a Musar book thousands of times, until he satisfied himself that he both understood it and lived in accordance with it.

His son-in-law, Rabbi Zvi Broide (not to be confused with Reb Yisrael's *rebbi* of the same name), described the Alter of Kelm as akin to a lion tamer. He was able to sustain his concentration without interruption for even an instant.

When Reb Yisrael left Kovno for Western Europe, in about 1858, Rabbi Simcha Zisl set out to nurture the Musar movement, much as Reb Yisrael had done when his own *rebbi*, Rabbi Yosef Zundel, left Salant for Jerusalem in 1838.

First, Rabbi Simcha Zisl taught children in Zager (Reb Yisrael's birthplace). Then he went to Moscow to be a mentor to Reb Yisrael's disciple who would become illustrious in business—Kalman Zev Wisotski, the tea manufacturer. After two years in Moscow, he returned to Kelm, in Lithuania, where his family lived, and founded a lay Musar group, which met weekly on the Sabbath.

By 1866, Rabbi Simcha Zisl had sufficiently thought through his pedagogic philosophy to found his own yeshiva, the Talmud Torah of Kelm. It was attended by boys up to 17, administered by the lay disciples in his Musar group, and assisted by Rabbi Nosson Zvi Finkel (later the Alter of Slobodka).

In 1876, minions of the Tsar maliciously (and ridiculously) accused the Alter of Kelm of plotting a revolution. He was able to escape by changing his last name from Broide to Ziv; and by moving his yeshiva from Kelm to Grubin, near the Baltic Sea.

By then the full force of the Alter's pedagogic power came to expression in a host of disciples who later became yeshiva deans and *mashgichim* throughout Eastern Europe. They included his own successors: his nephew Rabbi Zvi Broide, his son Rabbi Nachum Zev Broide, and Rabbi Reuven Dov Dessler (Reb Yisrael's grandson, the father of Rabbi Eliyahu Eliezer Dessler).

They included the likes of Rabbi Ben Zion Zev Krenitz, the first *mashgiach* in the Telshe yeshiva, and later the rabbi and founder of the yeshiva in Shveksena, a town near Telshe. Rabbi Krenitz was an epitome of Kelm Musar, an exalted specimen of humanity. His description by Rabbi Dov Katz conveys the richness of character and elegance of spirit that Kelm Musar could create:

> Rabbi Ben Zion Zev Krenitz was a model of Kelm in all its ornaments. He was pleasing physically: tall, elegant, handsome; meticulous in dress and entire appearance, wondrously controlled in every action, courteous and pleasant, his whole personality radiating charm and dignity. He was pleasing internally: overflowing with goodness and kindness, showing love and a friendly countenance to everyone; possessing exemplary qualities; noble in spirit and gentle in soul; aware of his purpose in life and marching confidently toward its realization; always working on himself—repairing, improving, ascending.

In Grubin, the Alter's health deteriorated. In 1881, he wrote to the aging Reb Yisrael, asking for permission to close the Talmud Torah. He was no longer able to lead and finance the institution, he said. Reb Yisrael staunchly refused. He said that the yeshiva's closure would be tantamount to the destruction of the *Beis Hamikdash*, the Holy Temple.

In about 1886, the Alter's vigor reached its end. Since Reb Yisrael (who died in 1883) had maintained that only the Alter was sufficiently wise to guide a yeshiva with secular studies, and since the Alter could not continue, he closed the Talmud Torah in Grubin and returned to Kelm.

By 1886, a Musar movement was under way. Musar yeshivas had begun to blossom, and the young Musar disciples who headed them urged their students to take the training under the ripened Alter of Kelm. With the closing of the Talmud Torah in Grubin, the most learned and sensitive in the Musar movement streamed to Kelm. The Alter's Beis Hatalmud, which since 1881 had been an informal gathering spot for his lay disciples, quickly reestablished itself as the major Musar yeshiva. Many of the rising stars who came to Kelm did so under the urging of Rabbi Nosson Zvi Finkel, whose Slobodka yeshiva was already a major third-generation Musar center.

From the Alter's return to Kelm in 1886 until his death in 1898, a galaxy of future yeshiva deans and *mashgichim* received training in Beis Hatalmud. To name a few (together with the locale of their subsequent leadership):

- Rabbi Isser Zalman Meltzer (Slobodka, Slutsk, Jerusalem);
- Rabbi Moshe Mordechai Epstein (Slobodka, Chevron);
- Rabbi Shlomo Zalman Dulinsky (Slobodka, Mir);
- Rabbi Leib Chasman (Telshe, Shetzutzin, Jerusalem);
- Rabbi Naftali Trop (Radin);
- Rabbi Sheftel Kramer (Slutsk, Cleveland).

Besides his own successors, others on whom Rabbi Simcha Zisl had had an earlier, decisive influence included:

- Rabbi Yosef Leib Bloch (Telshe);
- Rabbi Nosson Zvi Finkel, the Alter of Slobodka (Chapter 8);
- Rabbi Yosef Yozel Hurvitz, the Alter of Novorodock (Chapter 9).

Throughout their lives, the Alter and his wife, Sarah Leah, lived on a different, higher plane from the customary. These two Musar masters transcended needs that, to most people, seem indispensable.

The Alter never took a salary from the yeshivas he founded after his tutelage under Reb Yisrael; and he turned down the most lucrative rabbinic post in Russia, since he wished to be an educator. He and his wife earned a living as shopkeepers or laborers—for many years the Alter was a bookbinder—but theirs was a meagre living indeed.

Sometimes they literally had no bread on the table.

At one such time, when Sarah Leah Ziv was particularly desperate, her husband revealed that he had just come into 25 rubles (then a large sum). Fearing that he had taken the money as salary from the yeshiva that he himself had founded, she refused the money, desperate though she was. Only when the Alter assured her that his colleague, Reb Itzele Peterburger, had sent him the money for referring him to the rabbinic post in St. Petersburg did she she agree to accept the money.

Things did not have to be this way. The Alter could have taken a salary from his yeshiva. No one would have thought it improper. No one would have looked askance. But he and his wife did not wish to live from money that came to support yeshivas, even their own; and, they had *bitachon*, trust in Hashem.

The Alter, like all major Musar masters from Reb Yisrael down through the Alter of Novorodock and of Slobodka (and others), lived for long periods of time in accord with the halachic ideals of *perishus*, "separation," for Talmud scholars. The Alter of Kelm returned home from the yeshiva for Sabbath, festivals, and the eve of Passover (to perform *bedikas chometz*). In addition, he worked to "break his will": he never ate fruit soup, since he had once felt a lust for it; he never showed anger, unless he first put on a special garment; he always ate small fish after a fast, to discipline his appetite (many bones had to be carefully removed, a time-consuming task).

The purpose of the Alter's comprehensive *perishus*—self-control and suppression of selfishness—was to strive for heights in holiness and to share burdens with colleagues, even with all of humanity. As a person who devoted great energy to curbing his own desires, he shifted the focus of his concern from himself to the desires of others. Reducing his own needs, he had the time and the inclination to be sensitive to the needs of humanity.

Once a fire broke out in Kelm. The Alter ran to help extinguish it, even as he was halachically exempt on the principle that "he was an elder, and it was not in accord with his dignity." He wished to help others, exemption or no.

Although the Alter strove for solidarity with humanity, he did not, in his view, reach the required plateau. Once he was asked in a letter to pray for a sick person, and a sum of money was enclosed. He responded in a way that allows us to view his mind and heart—his careful learning, humility, and regard for universal solidarity.

> I am honored to be asked to pray for a sick person. But I am astonished. Whence did it occur to you that I consider myself to be a 'man of prayer,' and that I would, Heaven forbid, take money for this? Not a man of prayer am I.
>
> It is enough to remove myself from this, but, in order to clarify, here is what I would have to be, to be a 'man of prayer.' We have learned (*Shabbos* 67a):
>
> *If a tree casts its fruit, its owner paints it with red paint . . . But what remedy does this effect? When people see the red paint they will pray for the tree, that it bear fruit. . . . A person must make his anguish known publicly [by painting his tree red] that the public may seek Divine Mercy on his behalf.*
>
> Here we see the way of Torah. When a person sees someone else's property threatened, he must ask mercy from G-d, all the more so if someone else's health is threatened.
>
> We really must be astonished at how deeply rooted the love of humanity was in previous generations. Someone who simply saw a tree painted red knew why. Immediately he prayed for mercy, even though the tree's owner was nowhere in sight; for were the owner present, there would be no reason for the red paint. And money? The passers-by, who instinctively burst into prayer, certainly took none.
>
> From all this we learn that only when one bears the burdens of other people is his prayer efficacious.
>
> I am very far from this level of solidarity; and, Heaven forbid that I take money, which is hereby returned.

In selecting potential disciples, the Alter's primary criterion was their ability "to share the burdens of others without self-aggrandizement. When I find people like this, I naturally dedicate myself to them with soul-love."

If the Alter of Kelm had been a replica of Reb Yisrael Salanter, this would have been a failure of both *rebbi* and disciple. One of Reb Yisrael's major teachings was individuality. Each Musar student had to discover his own strengths and tasks. The Alter's colleague, Rabbi Naftali Amsterdam, once said regretfully to his *rebbi*, Reb Yisrael:

"If only I had the mind of the author of *Sha'agas Aryeh*; the heart of the author of *Yesod Veshoresh Ha'avodah*; and the qualities (*middos*) of the *rebbi* [Reb Yisrael himself]."

Reb Yisrael retorted sharply and affectionately:

"Naftali! With your *own* mind, your *own* heart, your *own middos*."

The Alter of Kelm differed from his master, as he should have. The Master—Reb Yisrael—sought to reach masses and individuals; the Alter, only individuals. The Master's vision was all encompassing; the Alter's, concentrated. The Master opened Musar teaching to all (albeit in varying degrees); the Alter, only to a select few. The Master traveled widely involving himself in communal problems in several countries; the Alter traveled little, involving himself in the intricate problems of disciples, regarding the learned, pious, and wise future leader to be a whole world. The Master was a visionary who often left details to others; the Alter built on the Master's vision to turn attention to detail into the nurture of scholar-leaders for the coming generation.

Reb Yisrael's grasp was hidden, above, beyond our own. The Alter's grasp, if also exalted, is nonetheless accessible. He left behind not only disciples but an educational philosophy. He transmitted a way to mold *adam hashalem*, the harmonious person of Torah.

"The whole world is a house of Musar and every human being is a book of Musar," the Alter used to say, summarizing his educational philosophy. All of life teaches Musar, teaches Torah, he taught.

But is not Torah itself sufficient? Is not the way to Torah to observe its commandments and study them? The Alter, answering in the affirmative, added clarifications.

First: Certain *mitzvos* or commandments of Torah are restricted to no particular time or place, and do not involve another human being or even a ritual object. Bachya ibn Pakuda, whose classic Musar work Rabbi Yehudah Leib Nekritz poured over his whole life, called such *mitzvos* "duties of the heart." Even prayer is excluded from these duties; it is called a "duty of the limbs," since it entails movement of the lips. Duties of the heart are wholly internal and continuously obligatory. One such *mitzvah* is to love Hashem. Another is to trust in Him, to have *bitachon*.

To fulfill the duties of the heart in all circumstances means that "the whole world is a house of Musar." The logic runs as follows: To be in the proper frame of mind to fulfill the wholly internal duties, such as trusting in Hashem, means that a person must have knowledge of all pitfalls that challenge *bitachon* or trust. To avoid these pitfalls, a person must be aware of them. To be aware of them, a person must know the world. He must know which circumstances to avoid, and which to embrace. He must treat the whole world as a place to learn Musar and each person as a teacher of Musar, for it is everywhere in the world and within every human encounter that a person must fulfill the duties of the heart, such as *bitachon*. Place and person reveal how best to observe a duty of the heart, and how worst to bungle it. Education in Torah thus takes place everywhere, said the Alter.

Second: All *mitzvos*, not only duties of the heart, are, though learned from the Torah, lived in people. To all Musar masters, stretching from Bachya (who lived some 900 years ago) to Rabbi Moshe Chaim Luzzatto (author of *Mesillas Yesharim, Path of the Upright*), down through Reb Yisrael and his disciples, every "duty of the limbs" requires both an objective deed and an internal response. Even those duties which are behavioral have an internal side. The observant Jew, the performer of Hashem's duties, must enable each and every one of them to transform his every fiber—his very being. He must enable *mitzvos* to turn him into an *eved Hashem*, a servant of G-d. He must understand that observance of *mitzvos* is *avodas Hashem*, service of G-d.

Now, to understand one's own psychological resistance to the all encompassing intent of *avodas Hashem*, and to overcome resistance, each person must understand his own circumstances and his own psyche. As the whole world is the arena in which Hashem's *mitzvos* are performed, each person must know how the world can help and hurt *mitzvah* performance. As the individual psyche is the arena in which each person must give his whole being to *avodas Hashem*, he must understand his psyche to purify it in relation to itself—to rid it of self-deception—and in relation to others—to rid it of selfishness and manipulation. "The whole world is a house of Musar and every human being is a book of Musar."

The Alter designed his educational philosophy to set his students in harmonious relationship with themselves, their families, their society—with the world. A tall order! Not everyone could succeed. Even those who could, could do so only with unceasing effort. This is why the Alter chose to work with students who seemed to have budding sensitivities (for solidarity, for example), and why he was unbending in his insistence on gradual, thorough progress in Musar. He distrusted sudden leaps of spirit, dramatic gestures, short-cuts.

To the Alter, no one was too talented to be exempt from gradual spiritual ascent. It is said of one of the celebrated sons of Kelm, Rabbi Yerucham Levovitz—later the *mashgiach* in the Mir yeshiva—that he wore his *tefilin* all day *for eighteen years* in order to learn to concentrate on one thing. (A man must concentrate on *tefilin* when wearing them.)

The key technique in molding the Musar personality was a special use of *sechel*, or intellect. To the Alter, there were layers of "intellectual action," of intellectual activity so acute that it triggered other human qualities. Intellectual activity, essential in building knowledge and character, did not accomplish these ends by itself. Step-by-step, *sechel* had to clothe itself (so to speak) in a spectrum of qualities that nurtured the *ba'al Musar* or Musar personality.

First: One learned to concentrate, to think with single-minded intensity for an extended period. This is what Rabbi Levovitz sought by wearing *tefilin* all day. This was intellectual activity.

Second: One learned to respond emotionally to concentrated intellectual activity.

Feeling and thinking went hand-in-hand.

Emotional response to thought—the first layer of "clothing" on *sechel*—was a contribution of the Musar movement. Elsewhere, in research for example, the search for documents, the rummaging in card catalogues, or the processing of experiments, diminishes the intensity of thinking. The thinking in Torah and Musar study can ascend to a duration and concentration so intense that it yields a unique human specimen: a person emotionally vibrant as well as intellectually acute, involved as well as erudite, down-to-earth and aristocratic. We need only recall Rabbi Ben Zion Zev Krenitz (described above) to know that the Alter of Kelm turned elevated theory into elevated people.

With reference to his Musar goal, the Alter said of his own *rebbi*: "Of course Darwin thought man descended from apes. He never saw Reb Yisrael."

Third: One learned to suffuse thinking and intellectually prompted emotion with *chiddush*, with an innovative turn of mind—the next layer added to pure intellect. In this way, individuality within the life of *mitzvos* went hand-in-hand with innovative insight.

Fourth: One learned to deepen individual insight into acquisition of the profundity of Torah, of the nature of one's personality, and of their interrelation. In and of itself, innovative insight, even if projected as "creativity," need not signal anything significant. As Rabbi Eliezer Ben Zion Bruk once sardonically told me: "People demand: Creativity! Creativity! A spider is very creative. It weaves the most intricate webs as if from nothing. What are they worth?"

The Musar personality's nurture of his own individuality must never let his creativity outstrip profound knowledge of Torah. The disciplined, sustained absorption of the immense quantity of Talmudic teaching is the necessary underpinning for the discovery of one's individuality. Here, as in every Musar task, brutal honesty is required, as the line between "Gehenna and the Garden of Eden is a mere hairsbreadth," said the Alter of Kelm. Creativity, *chiddush*? Yes, but only when it is built on knowledge; not when it is a rationalization for lack of discipline in Torah and Musar study.

In setting forth his educational philosophy—his program for nurturing *sechel*—the Alter set forth a lifelong program. He designed a pedagogic framework for the production of extraordinary leaders, for the perpetuation of the sublime piety and kindness that he witnessed in Reb Yisrael Salanter.

It is critical to look not only at the program's lofty heights, which can seem impossibly remote. It is necessary to recall that that yeshiva which commanded the Alter's best energy—the Talmud Torah in Grubin—was an elementary and a middle school. Many of the yeshiva deans, *mashgichim*, and educators who emerged from the Alter's watchful eye entered his care as children. For example, Reuven Dov Dessler, who became an epitome of Kelm Musar and, after the death of the Alter's son, the head of Kelm, arrived in Grubin when he was only 12. The Alter applied his lofty program to beginners slowly, surely, confidently.

Concentration? Begin by putting your mind to one thing for five minutes, said the Alter. Do not force yourself to begin with a longer period than you can naturally tolerate. *Take time.*

Then, gradually and steadily increase your concentration, a few minutes at a time. Always naturally—and always without skipping over difficult subjects. *Be exact.*

Then you will acquire the power to concentrate on difficult Talmudic subjects and Musar books, and on your character traits—on the large tasks in *avodas Hashem.* Gradually, you will acquire the ability to learn much Torah, and to change your nature.

Emotional responsiveness? Creative insight? Profound knowledge? Begin, simply, by *uncluttering the mind*, said the Alter. Put your mind to one text, and one personal trait, for five minutes. In concentrating on yourself, slowly but surely you rid yourself of *pizzur* or distractedness, of agitation without direction. As your concentration increases there gradually emerges in you more than knowledge.

There emerges serenity.

Slowly, gradually, but surely: serenity.

A peacefulness, a patience.

In deed, thought, and speech. From all this there begin to emerge in you the higher levels of emotion, creativity, and profundity.

You can hitch your vision to a star without being intimidated by the enormity of the task—assured the Alter—if you know that you have, and need, a lifetime to pursue it.

The Alter etched the patterns of Torah study and personal growth so carefully and strongly in the Beis Hatalmud of Kelm that when he died, in 1898, his major disciples sustained the yeshiva almost as if nothing had happened.

Reb Itzele Peterburger came to Kelm in *Elul* in the years immediately following the Alter's death to help compensate for the Alter's loss, but that is all he had to do: help. The Alter's disciples sustained Kelm with remarkable strength.

First to replace the Alter was his brother, Reb Leib Broide, who served three years, from 1898 until 1901, when he ascended to Jerusalem. Then came the Alter's *talmid muvhak* or preeminent disciple, Reb Leib's son Rabbi Zvi Broide, who led Bais Hatalmud from 1901 until his death in 1911; and then the Alter's own son, Rabbi Nachum Zev Broide, who led the yeshiva until his death in 1916.

In 1918, Rabbi Reuven Dov Dessler revived Kelm after the double ravage of Rabbi Nachum Zev's death and World War I. He was aided by Rabbi Nachum Zev's sons-in-law, Rabbis Daniel Movshovitz and Gershon Maideneck. They assumed the reigns of leadership in 1931 when Rabbi Dessler's health deteriorated and he moved to London to live with his son, Rabbi Eliyahu Eliezer Dessler. They led Kelm until its unspeakable destruction, and unbelievable heroism, with the onset of World War II.

The Alter's brother Reb Leib, who was many years younger than the Alter, was actually his disciple. By the time Reb Leib married, at 20, he was an expert in half the Talmud. Like his brother, Reb Leib never took money for studying or teaching Torah. He closed his business at noon each day to study—a schedule he never interrupted even when major commercial opportunities, offered in the afternoon, were lost. The Alter appreciated the special influence that Reb Leib's adherence to Kelm Musar—his punctuality and meticulousness in dress, honesty, and observance of *mitzvos*—wrought on the Gentiles and Jewish laymen with whom he dealt.

Reb Leib was the Alter's confidant, the recipient of many of the Alter's letters and articles which contain the Kelm system of Musar.

Reb Leib administered Beis Hatalmud for only a short time after his brother's death. Then, like other disciples of Kelm, he ascended to Jerusalem. He retained sufficient investments to live from the return, and gave the rest to his children. In Jerusalem he devoted himself entirely to Torah, Musar, prayer, and Kabbalah (on the texts of all of which he left manuscripts), until his death in 1928 at 94.

Reb Leib perpetuated the private strain of Musar that Reb Yisrael witnessed in Rabbi Yosef Zundel, partially sustained in himself, and nurtured in his own son, Rabbi Aryeh Leib Lipkin, and in his own *talmid muvhak*, Rabbi Naftali Amsterdam (Chapter 6).

The Alter's *talmid muvhak*, Reb Leib's son Rabbi Zvi Broide, was born in 1865. He grew to embody the finest in Kelm Musar: gentleness and friendliness, seriousness and studiousness, scrupulous regard for truth and integrity. On the last point, when he assumed the helm in Kelm in 1901, *he paid full board for the room he occupied in Beis Hatalmud*. Why should he be different from everyone else? Needless to add, he took no salary from the yeshiva. Independent, humble, he was the kind of person whom people wished to talk to. He made people comfortable. Friendly, serious, he would not let *anything* — a severe headache, a financial opportunity — distract him from his lengthy set times for Torah study. He operated his business a few hours daily, and that was all.

Rabbi Zvi Broide's humility and earnestness in Musar came to clearest expression in his *kabbalas* or resolutions.

Widespread in all schools of Musar, the writing of *kabbalas* enabled Musar seekers to identify goals and deficiencies. *Kabbalas* were written periodically to reflect the fine-tuning of the Musar student's progress, or lack thereof. I learned to undertake *kabbalas* from my teachers in Novorodock Musar, and I still do, each eve of Yom Kippur and Passover. In forcing myself to formulate my own spiritual and ethical goals and deficiencies, I have a better chance of carrying lofty intentions beyond the holy atmosphere of sacred times.

Here is one list of Rabbi Zvi Broide's *kabbalas* (slightly condensed):

1. *Truthfulness* — to take care to speak truth; to exclude untruth from one's affairs, for the more one rids oneself of falseness, the more that which remains stands out.

2. *Love* — to practice *chesed* or kindness with all Jews, especially with the sick and depressed, and always with a smile and understanding words.

3. *Thought* — to put the afterglow of the Sabbath to work in self-analysis; to identify, on Saturday night, the failures of the past week and the discipline for the coming week. In planning lies the success of man.

4. *Contemplation* — to search all deeds deeply.

5. *Constancy* — to raise to consciousness the obligation to be an *eved Hashem*, a servant of G-d; from the moment of awakening, to serve Him through body and soul.

6. *Restraint* — to curb pleasures, to break desires in times of suffering.

7. Five *shemuros:*
   • to guard the tongue, for all restraints are unequal to its force; life and death are its power.
   • to guard the eye.
   • to guard the heart.
   • to guard my prayers, lest they be lost to me.
   • to guard time, more precious than gold; to be a true *eved Hashem*, not to be lackadaisical.

8. *Review* — to read this list continually; at the very least, weekly.

9. *Deliberation* — not to act on impulse. Stop, think for a moment, what is the right course of action according to Jewish law and Musar in any undertaking, spiritual or worldly.

10. *Teaching* — to teach Musar daily. The purpose of Musar is to search one's business dealings, commitment to truthfulness, planning (or panic), eating, and lust in the heart.

The Alter's son, Rabbi Nachum Zev Broide, headed Beis Hatalmud after the death of his cousin, Rabbi Zvi Broide, in 1913. He joined the staff only three years earlier, having moved to Kelm from Koenigsberg.

Once a Polish rabbi arrived in Koenigsberg in need of medical treatment. Rabbi Nachum Zev approached him in *shul* and invited him home for tea. The Polish rabbi hesitated, doubtful whether the kitchen of this unknown Jew met the highest standards of *kashrus*. The rabbi finally accepted, figuring that here was an opportunity to learn about physicians in Koenigsberg.

The conversation stretched into the night. Rabbi Nachum Zev invited his guest to eat and sleep. Unhappy, without choice, the Polish rabbi agreed, and even then ate only dried foods.

In the middle of the night, the rabbi heard weeping in Rabbi Nachum Zev's room. He did not know what to think, and got out of bed. Standing near Rabbi Nachum Zev's door, he heard him repeating:

" '*Everything in your power to do, do; for there is neither initiative nor reckoning, neither knowledge nor wisdom, in she'ol [the grave], where you are headed*' " (Ecclesiastes 9:10).

The Polish rabbi then listened to a complete Musar *seder* or schedule of study, after which Rabbi Nachum Zev began to study Talmud in his sweet, alluring lilt until sunrise.

Only in the morning did the Polish rabbi learn the stature of his host, for "doing everything in your power" did not, according to Rabbi Nachum Zev, include informing people of one's knowledge and piety.

Rabbi Nachum Zev's study schedule the night of the Polish

rabbi's visit was typical. He rose regularly at 3:00 a.m. to study until morning prayers, after which he conducted business until 2:00 p.m., *never* later. The rest of the day he devoted to Torah study and communal affairs. Businessmen who arrived in Koenigsberg after 2:00 p.m. knew they had to wait until the next morning to see Rabbi Nachum Zev.

There is an extant picture of Rabbi Nachum Zev. It shows a stately individual, immaculately dressed, beard long and immaculately trimmed; a serenity suffusing the face—an earnest face, bodying forth an honesty, an integrity, both profound and simple. I have learned not to estimate the size of a *ba'al Musar* from pictures. Rabbi Eliezer Ben Zion Bruk, who was quite small, could loom large in a photograph. Perhaps Rabbi Nachum Zev was short, perhaps tall; either way, in his full length photograph, he appears massive and commanding.

His business, in lumber, often took him away from home. Even when traveling, his *seder* proceeded unchanged. His son-in-law, Rabbi Eliyahu Eliezer Dessler, remembered one long train ride from Kelm to Vilna, during which Rabbi Nachum Zev completed his schedule of study as though he were sitting comfortably in a yeshiva or in the quiet of his home.

Rabbi Nachum Zev looked like a lumberman, was taken to be a lumberman, but underneath the exterior was an unusual person who enjoyed the lack of attention that so easily could have been his.

> Once, at a wedding celebration, the first speaker—an honored citizen of Vilna—fumbled his speech. Rabbi Nachum Zev, an outstanding orator, was scheduled to speak next, but refused. He later told disciples that he did not wish to stand out at the expense of the first speaker.

We have, here, a critical lesson in the Kelm conception of humility. Rabbi Nachum Zev knew that he would have outshone the previous speaker: humility is not denying who one is. It is not self-derogation, not "putting oneself down." Rabbi Nachum Zev's humility was in not calling attention to himself at another person's expense; in fact, in not calling attention to himself at all. Humility is double honesty: *I know that I outshine someone else in a certain respect; I also know that Hashem outshines me infinitely, so on what basis am I permitted to call attention to myself?*

Every Sunday Rabbi Nachum Zev would visit hospitals. He visited friends and strangers alike. He acquired medical knowledge in order to guide people in their recovery. At times, physicians would consult with him on strictly medical issues. He became a familiar face in hospitals, with his stately demeanor and neat carrying case, always filled with kosher food for patients. Once he wrote his father, the Alter, that two things especially strengthened him: his father's letters, and his visits to hospitals.

We have, here, a critical lesson in Kelm Musar. It is not simply giving, "being an idealist." Rabbi Nachum Zev knew that he himself gained from his hospital visits. He learned to appreciate life and health. He learned to curb his personal desires in order to free himself to help others. Musar, then, is both giving and gaining. But, for both, there is an important proviso. One must help people in the way they need to be helped. Sometimes, helpers, feeling pain at someone else's suffering, set out to alleviate, really, not the pain of the sufferer, but their own. In doing so, they risk losing the necessary objectivity to provide the sufferer with the help he actually needs. Because Rabbi Nachum Zev gave properly, he gained properly. His joy in helping others was legitimate because he helped *them*, not himself.

But in helping *them*, he did help himself. He brought joy and insight to himself.

That is Kelm Musar.

Although the behavior of third and fourth generation Musar disciples during World War II is rightly classified as a type of Holocaust heroism, as "spiritual resistance," the classification of this behavior exclusively as a Holocaust phenomenon robs it of its particularity. To Musar masters, the Holocaust was simply a more acute challenge to the goals they had long received from their teachers.

In 1941, Rabbi Daniel Movshovitz, successor to Rabbi Reuven Dov Dessler as head of Beis Hatalmud, found himself together with the Jews of Kelm face-to-face with machine guns at the foot of a death pit.

Rabbi Daniel asked the German officer in command of the killing operation to allow him to say some parting words to his flock. The officer agreed, but ordered the rabbi to cut it short.

As though he were delivering one of his regular lectures to his students, Rabbi Daniel spoke quietly and calmly about *kiddush Hashem*—giving one's life rather than forfeiting one's faith. After he had spolen a while, the German shouted at him to finish.

He turned to his Jews. He said:

"Behold, we have now reached the point about which I have spoken just now: *kiddush Hashem*, Sanctification of the Divine Name. Therefore, do not be confused; accept the decree without panic."

Then he turned to the German. He said:

"I have finished. You can begin."

That is Kelm Musar.

6.

Rabbis Yitzchak Blazer and Naftali Amsterdam

"With His goodness, He renews each day, all the time, the works of creation."

Thus a Jew prays each day.

With His goodness, Hashem sustains and guides all life, all the time.

Nothing is accident.

Nothing small, nothing big.

The timing in writing this book had me pen the introduction to Rabbi Yitzchak Blazer—"Reb Itzele Peterburger"—in the month of *Elul*, the time before Rosh Hashanah.

"The whole year should be taken as *Elul*," said Reb Yisrael

Salanter. "Nevertheless, *Elul* is *Elul*."

Elul is special.

Elul is different.

Elul compels the prospect of standing face to face before the King of Kings. It strips away defenses and excuses for failure and levity—spiritual failure and unrestrained joy.

There is a time for seriousness, and a time for joy, not that the two are not ultimately, and mutually, related.

But not now.

Not in *Elul*.

Now is the time for reevaluation, for introspection, for examining patterns of the past.

It is the time for examining the person who, in his day, was called "the master of all the Diaspora" in *yir'as Hashem* — the person who understood most deeply, and could teach most poignantly, what it meant to stand before the King of Kings in all seasons, at all times.

Accident? Coincidence?

No.

In the countless decisions that make up life — that determine schedules — it was meant, through His goodness, that I reach this time to write about this man, the master of *yir'as Hashem*.

Reb Itzele Peterburger.

In the lore that has filtered its way through memories and lapses of history—stories forgotten, documents lost, pious deeds hidden from the chonicler's pen—we receive the teaching that Reb Yisrael Salanter had three major disciples: the Alter of Kelm, "sage" (*chacham*); Reb Itzele Peterburger, "scholar" (*lamdan*); and Rabbi Naftali Amsterdam, "saint" (*tzaddik*).

This is true.

But it is also not true, in the sense that there were other disciples who might have ranked with these three had they lived a normal span; in the sense that it is pointless to ponder superfine distinctions between disciples who achieved lofty levels of Torah learning and piety; in the sense that there were, I am convinced, disciples who, like Reb Yisrael in Germany, hid their piety so well that history could not capture it.

And so, as we ponder Reb Itzele, "the second major disciple of Reb Yisrael," let us keep in mind the limitations of all such classifications.

Reb Itzele was born in 1837 in a small suburb of Vilna. His family was poor. The sustenance of his youth was Torah study, sometimes literally, as food was simply unavailable. He married at 15, settled in Kovno, and studied under Reb Yisrael.

He never wished to live from his learning, and learned to be a painter. But Reb Yisrael, seeing his talent, urged him to enter the rabbinate. In 1862—when he was only 25—he assumed one of the most prestigious posts in all of Russia, Rabbi of St. Petersburg (now Leningrad), capital of Tsarist Russia. In 1867—at age 30—he completed his large halachic work, *Peri Yitzchak*. Much later, the solidity of this work and the character of its author came to the attention of the Rabbi of Brisk, Yosef Dov Halevi Soloveitchik (1820-1897).

At a meeting of great Talmudic scholars in St. Petersburg, which Rabbi Soloveitchik chaired, he posed a *kushiyyah* (a difficult Talmudic problem) in the name of his illustrious son and successor, Rabbi Chaim Soloveitchik. A storm of learned proposals and counterproposals raged through the gathering, each scholar demonstrating his acuity and erudition, only to have it challenged.

Reb Itzele Peterburger sat silent.

Finally, Rabbi Soloveitchik quieted the crowd—transcended the arguments—with two penetrating resolutions, one of his own and one in the name of his son. When the meeting broke up, he wondered how Reb Itzele, who had not even seemed to follow the discussion, had acquired his reputation as a first-rank scholar. Rabbi Soloveitchik asked to have *Peri Yitzchak* brought to him. He thumbed through it, to evaluate the erudition of its author.

Suddenly, abruptly, he came to a halt.

He read in *Peri Yitzchak* the very question or *kushiyyah* his son had posed.

Then he read two resolutions.

His own, and that of his son.

And Reb Itzele had sat silent.

He knew how to humble himself.

He was so humble, said Reb Yisrael, that he did not know that he was humble.

"**G**olus." *Praven golus.*

A concept so foreign to most people that it takes a special effort of the imagination to counter instinctive recoil at its extremities, let alone to appreciate the greatness of soul and loftiness of aspiration of the people who lived it.

Golus.

Literally: *Exile.*

A moving away, geographically, from all that is familiar. A self-exile; travels to places where no one knows you, where you know no one. Travels by foot, and without money, without destination or hope of comfort.

Without stability, or routine.

Without the familiar.

Reb Itzele and his childhood friend, Rabbi Naftali Amsterdam, used to *praven golus.* As common beggars, they wandered from hamlet to hamlet in Lithuania. They sought to know the soul of the beggar—to know it existentially, experientially.

They waited in line at the end of *ma'ariv* (the evening prayer) on Friday night, hoping that someone would invite them for a Sabbath meal.

They sat at beggars' tables.

They ate leftovers.

They learned what it was like to feel totally dependent, totally at mercies beyond their power, for the barest necessities.

Golus was an exercise.

A Musar exercise.

They learned to deepen, to render constant, their sense of dependence on Hashem. Living as beggars, simulating dependence on others, they nurtured a sense that could be transposed to their spiritual aspiration to feel totally at the mercy, totally under the care—the felt concern—of the Holy One, Blessed be He.[1]

It took a great soul, to begin with, to subject himself to the deprivation of *golus*; even more, to imagine the *magregas*, the spiritual levels, yet needed to be attained after one was already a great scholar and *anav* (humble person).

Reb Itzele had that imagination.

Should Reb Itzele remain Rabbi of St. Petersburg?

There was honor.

There was position.

There was a very handsome salary.

In 1878, Reb Itzele resigned.

He had served 16 years—it was enough.

We may imagine that this position went against his grain.

There were unpleasant tasks (such as entering churches to obtain names of apostates [*mumarim*] needed for bills of divorce).

There were the pomp and ceremony—for him, irritants.

There was the separation from his comrades—from his entire nurture, the Torah Jewry of Lithuania.

But in one respect Reb Itzele's subsequent career with the Musar movement was an extension of his life as Rabbi of St. Petersburg. Throughout, Reb Itzele embraced responsibility.

He was a man of initiative, new projects, and fresh horizons.

---

1. David Zaritsky, in *Gesher Tzar*, his biographical novel of Rabbi Yosef Yozel Hurvitz (the Alter of Novorodock), memorably captures Reb Itzele and Rabbi Amsterdam in their *golus*, particularly in a poignant re-imagining of the incident when Reb Itzele was invited by the parents of one of his disciples. Imagine: the shock on the disciple's face at seeing his *rebbi*—the respected, the renowned, the revered Reb Itzele Peterburger!—acting as, and being treated as, a common beggar. The disciple instinctively let out a shriek of recognition and set out to remedy the situation, only to be stopped in his tracks with a slight but stern gesture from Reb Itzele, signaling the confused young man to be silent.

The *golus* proceeded.

He was an indefatigable organizer, traveler, administrator, polemicist, preacher, fundraiser, counselor, teacher—all on behalf of Torah and Musar. If the Alter of Kelm settled in but two places—Kelm and Grubin—to nurture major centers of Musar, Reb Itzele moved across Lithuania and beyond, seizing every opportunity to bring encouragement to a new Musar institution or to bolster an old one.

- In 1878, upon returning to Kovno from St. Petersburg, he delivered impassioned Musar talks in the *batei Musar* founded by Reb Yisrael.

- In 1881, he became dean of the Kovno *Kolel*—the first yeshiva for married men—founded three years earlier by Reb Yisrael and by the Rabbi of Kovno, Yitzchak Elchanan Spektor. In this position, Reb Itzele assisted in the founding of several branches of the *Kolel* in surrounding towns.

- Also in about 1880, he assisted in the founding of the Slobodka yeshiva. He provided moral support and funding, and delivered Musar talks and Talmudic lectures.

- In the 1880s he administered a large Torah fund, established by Ovadiah Lachman, which supported, among other institutions, the Kovno *Kolel*.

- In 1896 to 1897, he assisted in founding six early centers of Novorodock Musar.

- In 1897, when a rebellion against Musar study from within the Slobodka yeshiva led to its split into the Kaminetz ("Knesses Beis Yitzchak") and Slobodka ("Knesses Beis Yisrael") yeshivas, he assisted in getting the weakened Slobodka yeshiva back on its feet.

- In 1898, when Rabbi Simcha Zisl died, he spent the 40 days from the beginning of *Elul* to Yom Kippur in Kelm, and returned for this period the next two years. He helped to maintain Kelm with his Musar talks and his presence.

- On his way to *Eretz Yisrael* in 1903, he passed through Vilna, where Rabbi Chaim Ozer Grodzinski and the Chafetz Chaim begged him to stay. He did, for a year-and-a-half, garnering support for *Kolel Vilna-Zamot* in Jerusalem.

- In 1904, when he finally ascended to Jerusalem, he helped to bolster the *beis ha-Musar* in the Strauss Courtyard, and to administer *Kolel Vilna-Zamot*. He was offered the post of Rabbi of Jerusalem (he turned it down).

Amid all this activity—administering and teaching, self-scrutinizing and *golus*, controversy and silence—there was a story, a human story, to Reb Itzele.

The story begins with clues—large clues, for someone else, but not for him. One clue was the voluntary nature of his public service. When he resigned as Rabbi of St. Petersburg—and thence onward—he took no money for any of his organizational duties, stretching over a period of 29 years.

Selflessness.

When he prepared for *Simchas Torah* in his old age, he needed a doctor present, to make certain he not overdo it. From his energetic and enthusiastic dancing, he had to change shirts several times in the course of the day.

Youthfulness.

When he prepared for Purim, he reminded himself of Reb Yisrael's interpretation of the obligation *livesumei — to drink —* until one knows no difference between "Blessed is Haman" and "Cursed is Mordechai": the obligation is to drink. The means of reaching ignorance about Haman and Mordechai is the *mitzvah*, not the ignorance itself. And so, he used to carry on and about in unrestrained joy, singing and dancing in the streets of Kovno.

The one who was the master of fear of Heaven was the master of joy—at the appropriate time. When he prayed during *Elul* and the Ten Days of Repentance, "the dread of Hashem fell over him," as Rabbi Dov Katz put it. "He was observed quaking—literally quaking—before the coming reckoning. They used to say: Whoever has not seen Reb Itzele Peterburger during the Days of Awe has never seen awe in his life. His prayer shocked. It was full of quiet weeping. Anyone who heard it, quaked."

The one who was the master of joy was the master of fear of Heaven.

Agility.

Richness of spirit.

And these are only, for him, clues.

Amid all this activity—spiritual and physical—there unfolded a human story of suffering, sensitivity—and serenity.

Reb Itzele and his wife were childless.

Under Halachah, Reb Itzele could have divorced his wife after ten years of childlessness.

Under the mores of the time, Reb Itzele could have readily exercised his halachic right.

He did not.

He did not even mention the right.

He and his wife remained married, and childless, for 35 years.

And Reb Itzele sat silent.

After 35 years, his wife offered to be divorced, and Reb Itzele divorced her (he supported her the rest of her life).

He remarried a young widow with four children.

He raised them as his own. He trained them, educated them, saw them to the marriage canopy.

He and his second wife had four children.

He diapered them, arose in the middle of the night whenever they cried, and helped with the household chores, especially on the eve of Sabbath—even when he was an old man.

If ever there were situations—spiritual or physical—when his eight children could not be treated equally, he favored his adopted children, for they were orphans, and "an orphan and a widow do not oppress."

So the story goes: the time Reb Itzele forgot to take leave of the housekeeper before departing for his 40-day silence, the special letter he sent to ask her pardon; the time as an old man he lent his presence to the wedding of a stranger who had never studied Torah and then decided to do so, as his presence would be an encouragement, an act of kindness; the times he sat silent when *maskilim* slandered him; the time just before his death, in 1907, when he instructed that no eulogies be recited for him.

Small kindnesses, small acts of character—the small perfections which constitute building blocks of a monumental life.

Reb Itzele Peterburger lived fully: in joy, in dread, in care and concern, in learning and love.

Through himself he lived for others, for the Musar tradition, for Torah, for the Master of the World.

Reb Itzele Peterburger.

An induplicable presence.

Rabbi Naftali Amsterdam

Rabbi Naftali Amsterdam left a will with seven provisions. Six dealt with spiritual and halachic matters. Only one dealt with money because he died with virtually no money and no property.

In the sixth provision, Rabbi Naftali wrote:

"A person must refashion improper traits, and for this two things are needed. One: Musar study. Two: a good friend, *especially* a good friend."

To history, Rabbis Simcha Zisl Ziv (the Alter of Kelm), Itzele Peterburger, and Naftali Amsterdam were the three major disciples of Reb Yisrael Salanter.

To appreciative contemporaries, these three were *tzaddikim.*

To each other, they were friends.

They met in Kovno in the 1850s. Their friendship was forged on several levels: they shared the same *rebbi;* they shared the same ideals; they shared a genuine affection for each other.

Rabbi Naftali would share an *Elul* with Rabbi Simcha Zisl—then write Reb Itzele about it. Rabbi Simcha Zisl would miss an opportunity to spend time with Rabbi Naftali—then Rabbi Simcha Zisl would express his disappointment in a letter to Reb Itzele. Reb Itzele would plan a memorial volume for Reb Yisrael (*Or Yisrael*, 1900) and ask Rabbi Naftali to participate—Rabbi Naftali's memoir issued promptly. Rabbi Naftali and Reb Itzele set out on *golus*—together. Rabbi Simcha Zisl died—Reb Itzele rushed to Kelm to help fill the void . . . the incidents of friendship multiply endlessly.

Genuine friendship, a human need and a precious achievement, is also a Musar necessity. The individual human mind, or soul, cannot successfully be its own mirror in assessing its religious (particularly its *humanly* religious) weaknesses. Glory-seeking or jealousy, malicious speech or manipulation—interpersonal vices of any kind, interpersonal violations of Torah on any level—fall prey to blindness or rationalization in attempts to analyze and overcome them.

A genuine friend who is also a Musar partner provides a control—a fresh and helpful angle of vision—that one's own mind can only partially provide.

" . . . this good friend," wrote Rabbi Naftali in his will, "work with him at special times to refashion improper traits. Seek with him means to accomplish this."

Elsewhere, Rabbi Naftali elaborated:

"Good friends, Musar friends, will point out to each other virtues and vices, for the purpose of identifying a realizable good. . . . The truth is that when a person isolates himself from trustworthy friends, from Musar friends, sluggishness and temptation overcome him. He forgets his obligations and the obstacles in his nature. A good friend awakens him."

Rabbi Naftali's good friends (besides awakening him) transmitted his legacy. It had to be that way, for Rabbi Naftali revealed virtually nothing about himself, except to them. He became the conduit for the side of Reb Yisrael Salanter that resembled Rabbi Yosef Zundel—the conduit for hidden *avodas Hashem*.

The family background of Rabbi Naftali is unknown. His parents apparently occupied no special station. He needed no benefit of lineage or example, of social standing or intellectual expectation, to become what he became. All differences allowed, he was akin to a contemporary *ba'al teshuvah* in that he radically exceeded expectations. He ascended to heights far beyond those to be predicted on the basis of his background.

He was born in 1832. As a youth he was a *masmid*, dedicated to Talmud study. As a teenager, it seems that he was already studying under Reb Yisrael Salanter, in Vilna. With Reb Yisrael's move to Kovno, young Naftali (not even 20) moved to the core of Reb Yisrael's attention. Much later, Reb Yisrael, who was very restrained in his use of titles, termed Rabbi Naftali a "great man" (*adam gadol*) in Torah and *yir'ah*.

Rabbi Naftali studied with awesome concentration all day long — standing. He achieved complete recall of the entire Talmud and *Shulchan Aruch*, Code of Jewish Law.

He sustained his intellectual drive into his forties, when he served as Rabbi of Helsingfors and *dayyan* in St. Petersburg. His mind was ordered; his oratory, lucid; his writing, coherent. His public abilities were noteworthy, but his heart was elsewhere.

Hidden service of Hashem.

Purity, purity — it required all of his heart, all of his soul.

In Rabbi Naftali's search for ever higher levels of purity, there was not a shred of complacency. His search had an urgency, a ceaseless urgency.

Generations did not phase him. Rabbi Binyamin Zilber wishes to reach back to the *madregah* of Reb Yisrael, at least of Reb Itzele. Rabbi Naftali wished to reach back to the *madregah* of Rabbi Yosef Karo and of *Sh'lah*. "When will I reach my goal?" he asked, plaintively.

"I have failed, like a person walking down the path — snow on one side, fire on the other — as my soul is always in turbulence. When will I reach my goal, the lofty plateau, the sacred path trod by holy ones of earlier generations — *Beis Yosef* (Rabbi Yosef Karo) and *Sh'lah*? They ascended. They walked with G-d, in levels of separation and solitude, in Torah for its own sake — all this, in all its detail."

My soul is always in turbulence. Why? "Behold, in these times, the promptings of the soul, the arousals of the soul, are great."

Turbulence, to Rabbi Naftali: not spiritual self-enclosure. *Purity:* not a selfish pursuit, not flight from this world. For *in these times* the promptings of the soul overflow.

In these times.

Rabbi Naftali's passionate, ceaseless search to bring to realization the lofty plateaus of earlier and greater servants of Hashem was for the purpose of bringing an essential cure, an essential tranquillity, to his times, his generation.

Rabbi Naftali sought to return his whole generation to righteousness.

Thus did he write in a private notation, and in a letter to one of his friends, Reb Itzele Peterburger.

"**T**o *return his whole generation to righteousness."*
Is this grandiose, illusionary?

The revolution that Reb Yisrael Salanter attempted to set in motion was comprehensive. It was not a revolution of ideas alone — of a book or two, a disciple or two, or even a yeshiva or two. Each person who came under Reb Yisrael's influence became an integral part of a plan that sought to bring a revitalized Judaism to all corners of Jewish life.

A critical clue to the breadth of Reb Yisrael's aspirations was the hold he had over his disciples. The idea of the preeminent Talmud scholar as the national leader — the counselor on all matters, large and small, communal and personal — originated with Reb Yisrael. And so, when Rabbi Naftali was in his thirties, we find him, under the impact of Reb Yisrael's encouragement, altering his own aspirations in a major way.

We have here a very subtle combination.

On the one hand, Reb Yisrael had to advise Rabbi Naftali in accord with his own personal strengths. The Musar teaching demanded that each person fulfill "*his* obligation in *his* world." On the other hand, Reb Yisrael had to find a way to integrate the individual strengths of Rabbi Naftali into the larger picture that he envisioned for *klal Yisrael* — the picture of how to return a generation to righteousness.

When Rabbi Naftali's family grew, when the burden of the necessary livelihood became impossible for his wife to bear alone,

Rabbi Naftali decided: I shall become a baker. And Reb Yisrael said: No!

It was not that Reb Yisrael was insensitive to material need, on either a philosophical or a practical plane. Philosophically, he said (in one of his pungent aphorisms): "Spiritual needs are more important than physical needs, but another person's physical needs are my own spiritual obligation." Practically, Reb Yisrael often advised against *perishus* (separation from worldly endeavor) — he advised the Alter of Novorodock against this, for example — and he was always sensitive to the financial side of a spiritual matter. We may recall, for example, his understanding of the need to send funds for a new horse to the would be suicide whom he counseled under the bridge in Vilna. In Rabbi Naftali's case, however, Reb Yisrael discerned that his remarkable disciple, richly endowed in spiritual and intellectual talent, would fail his destiny by turning to baking. Reb Yisrael knew that Rabbi Naftali was capable of the high level of *bitachon* that could insure his livelihood. He also knew that, with additional study and growth, he would assume the stature to hold a respectable rabbinic post.

This, then, was the background to Rabbi Naftali's assumption of rabbinic posts in Helsingfors and elsewhere — not the post of baker — when financial need pressed excessively.

It is also the background to Rabbi Naftali's limiting his terms as a salaried, rabbinic employee to an absolute minimum, and devoting the preponderance of his years to hidden service of Hashem.

Hidden service of Hashem was his unique talent.

It was his unique contribution to Reb Yisrael's multifaceted plan to "return the generation to righteousness."

Accordingly, it was not grandiose, but consistent with Rabbi Naftali's makeup and destiny for him to desire to bring an essential cure, an essential righteousness, to his times.

How does this work? Does not a hidden *tzaddik*, by definition affect no one but himself? Not really. To begin with, in

Judaism there is no such thing as an absolutely hidden *tzaddik*. Now matter how reclusive, a *tzaddik* must still pray with a *minyan*. He must still trade in *divrei Torah* (words of Torah) with other scholars. He must still have friends. If in these contexts alone, the hidden *tzaddik* has an impact. He has a presence. He has a way of attracting similarly pure souls. Rabbi Yosef Zundel attracted Reb Yisrael. Rabbi Yosef Zundel, "hidden unto the vessels" (*nechbah el hakelim*), released his G-d-intoxication into the world through his disciple, Reb Yisrael Salanter.

It is a paradox.

Turning inward, the hidden *tzaddik* guarantees the generation of forces for purity which reach outward.

This is how it happened with Reb Yosef Zundel.

This is how it happened with Rabbi Naftali.

We do not know precisely how it happened with Rabbi Naftali. We cannot trace it as we can with Rabbi Yosef Zundel. But we do not need to know how a *tzaddik* leaves his imprints. A *tzaddik* will leave them. Rabbi Naftali left them. It is impossible for it to have been otherwise.

And we do have clues.

We know, for example, that Rabbi Naftali had a strong impact on the young and receptive Reb Aryeh Levin, "a *tzaddik* in our time." Reb Aryeh left an indelible imprint on the life of twentieth-century Jerusalem. He was a man who built receptivity among avowed Israeli secularists — on a level presently unappreciated — to the idea of *teshuvah*. This idea is now moving through Israeli society with an intensity wholly unpredictable in 1969, when Reb Aryeh died. Obviously, Israeli *teshuvah* is a complex development; obviously, Reb Aryeh's own development was complex. It was complex, though, only in the diversity of pietistic influences upon its fertile receptivity to piety.

Was Rabbi Naftali the decisive influence?

Perhaps, perhaps not. But he was an influence, and so the point is the same: the imprints upon the soul of the *tzaddik* who changes society are left by other *tzaddikim*, one or several, public or private.

Rabbi Naftali left imprints.

Rabbi Naftali turned others deeply to righteousness.

The only historian who can trace this in all its precision, all its fullness, is the Historian.

That is enough.

A hidden *tzaddik*, like Rabbi Naftali, affected far more than himself; he affected his world. We need not know how. Hashem knows.

That is enough.

Rabbi Naftali was a *gadol beyir'ah*, "a great man in fear of Heaven," said Reb Yisrael.

What did Reb Yisrael mean?

A clue:

On Purim, Rabbi Naftali used to carry on in a manner akin to Reb Itzele: drinking quite a bit, loosening up, telling stories. He came out from behind his veil of privacy in the free and uninhibited manner that is unique to Purim — he let himself go.

Such behavior, one might think, is the last place to look for the secret to fear of Heaven.

But look at *Psalms*.

Psalms 100:2 commands: "*Serve Hashem with joy (simchah)*."

Psalms 2:11 commands: "*Serve Hashem with fear (yir'ah)*."

A contradiction?

Not at all. Fear of Heaven is the central quality that Hashem praises, that Hashem wishes his people to acquire. Abraham, our Father, just after his great test in the binding of Isaac, is told by Hashem: "Now I know that you are a *yir'ei Elohim*, one who fears G-d." King David, reflecting upon his rescue from pursuers, exclaims: "How great is the goodness You have stored up for those who fear You." The Rosh Hashanah prayer book has all Jews beseech Hashem: "Let all humanity fear You."

In fear of Heaven, a person's priorities are in order. In fear of doing the wrong thing, fruitless byways and wrong desires, sin and selfishness, are banished. A person's perspectives are correct. Overwhelmed by the prospect of Divine punishment and the awesomeness of Divine majesty, a person who fears Heaven stands before the

Creator of the universe, knowing that his task is to do His will. Nothing else is important, *and therefore nothing else bothers him.*

In fear of Heaven there is perfect tranquillity.

And in perfect tranquillity there is *simchah*, joy.

Undisturbed in doing what he is supposed to do—the will of Hashem—a person is full of joy.

There is no contradiction between "serving Hashem with fear" and "serving Hashem with joy" because fear is the foundation of joy. In Rabbi Naftali's self-nullification before Hashem, in his utter fear and awe of Hashem—of Hashem alone—he knew tranquillity. He knew serenity. He knew *simchah—simchah shel mitzvah*—in everything he did.

And so, when Hashem's command was to behave in a way that society conventionally characterizes as joyful—in drinking and personal release—Rabbi Naftali was fit and ready to meet the task. Purim, whose "face" is joy, and Rosh Hashanah, whose "face" is fear, drew ready responses from Rabbi Naftali. Strikingly different on the surface, *simchah* and *yir'ah* drew from the same well, in Rabbi Naftali.

In a person in whom fear of Heaven is the stream of life, serving Hashem with fear and serving Him with joy flow together as naturally as merging mountain streams.

Which is why Purim, no less than the occasions of Rabbi Naftali's seriousness, is a clue to his greatness in *yir'ah*; which is why Reb Yisrael called Rabbi Naftali an *adam gadol* in *yir'ah*.

And which, too, is why Reb Itzele Peterburger was a great man. He and his friend, his human friend and his Musar friend—the two *golus* vagabonds—successfully nullified from consciousness every distraction, every temptation, everything except *yir'as Hashem*.

They were full of fear and awe of Hashem.

And: full of *simchah*.

Fear of Hashem and joy in Hashem are ultimately, and mutually, related.

Psalms 2:11: "Rejoice with trembling"—before Hashem. Rejoice and tremble—both. Joy and fear—both.

Together.

7.

First-Generation Disciples in the Musar Movement

Reb Yisrael admitted to the circle of his concern more than disciples who could perpetuate his unique Musar teaching, in all its fullness. He admitted more than Rabbis Simcha Zisl Ziv, Itzele Peterburger, and Naftali Amsterdam.

Reb Yisrael Salanter raised up disciples who occupied a wide variety of positions of spiritual and communal leadership: the yeshiva dean, the *parush* (ascetic), the lay leader, the *maggid* (preacher), and the patron of Musar.

He reached out to such Jews as Reb Leizer Gordon, Reb Abramchik Tanis, Rabbi Elinka Kartinger, the *Maggid* of Kelm, and Reb Shraga Feivel Frank—Jews who brought to their tutelage under

Reb Yisrael a distinct orientation already formed by circumstance, inclination, or instruction.

With these Jews Reb Yisrael infused capable personalities—their given orientation, already formed—with a Musar perspective. He broadened diverse talents to include the propagation of the Musar wisdom. As such, he fortified the Musar movement by broadening its base.

If some disciples captured Reb Yisrael's teaching in all its fullness, and others captured it partially, all contributed to its authority and acceptance.

Each of the following disciples turned a distinctive spiritual or communal role to the service of the Musar movement.

Yeshiva Dean

When Reb Yisrael came to Kovno in 1848 or 1849, the phenomenon of founding a new yeshiva was just that—a phenomenon. In our time, the founding of a yeshiva is a sign of strength because it counters a weakness, assimilation. But in Reb Yisrael's time, the founding of a yeshiva in Lithuania could be seen as a sign of weakness. What purpose could a new yeshiva serve? Was not everyone already studying Torah in the myriad of local synagogues, *shtiblech* and *batei midrash*? Were not there already yeshivas for advanced students?

Why a new yeshiva?

The question made sense if the analysis that the religious foundations of Lithuanian Jewish society were sound was correct. Reb Yisrael thought not. He thought that while all appeared to be sound on the surface, the foundations were crumbling. *Haskalah* and mandatory military conscription (for 31 years!) would radically erode religious commitment, he predicted, unless new and bold steps were taken.

And so, he founded a new yeshiva in Kovno.

But this was not enough.

Reb Yisrael would also have to found *founders* of new yeshivas. This he did in raising up Rabbi Simcha Zisl Ziv, who founded the Musar yeshiva in Kelm, and Rabbi Itzele Peterburger, who, as a general organizer, had a hand in founding several yeshivas and *kolelim* in and around Kovno, Slobodka, and Novorodock.

All these yeshivas had an intensive Musar program and tone. But this was not enough.

Reb Yisrael knew that some yeshivas would be less innovative, more "mainstream"; that some yeshiva deans would likewise be less innovative, more "mainstream. " He knew that he would have to place his stamp on these yeshivas, and yeshiva deans, too. In Kovno, it was his genius to spot a young boy who had the threefold capacity to master the Talmud, to communicate the process of that mastery, and to love the nurture of the institution for Talmudic learning: the yeshiva.

Eliezer Gordon, born near Vilna in 1841, was this boy—the future founder and *rosh yeshiva* (yeshiva dean) of Telshe.

Utterly fearless, also utterly compassionate, especially to his students, Reb Leizer Gordon's *bris milah* or circumcision was a metaphorical portent of all that was to come.

> There was no *mohel* or ritual circumcizer in the village in which he was born. Traveling by night in wintertime over bumpy country roads in a wood-wheeled wagon, the week-old baby bounced out of the wagon. None of the passengers noticed. When finally they did notice, they turned back in panic to search for him. Whey they spotted him, a wolf was sniffing at him from every side, but did him no harm. Little Eliezer Gordon grew to manhood with the fearlessness of a wolf—a quality he put to good use in building the yeshiva and the community of Telshe—even as he harmed no one.

Reb Leizer Gordon's rise was phenomenal. Perhaps he was 12, perhaps 14, when he arrived in Reb Yisrael's yeshiva in Kovno. Reb Yisrael immediately perceived his potential. Within a few years Reb Yisrael appointed him chief lecturer (*maggid shiur*) of a class for rabbis-in-training. So as not to kindle jealousy among the students, Reb Yisrael designated Reb Leizer Gordon to lecture every other week, with Reb Yisrael himself delivering the *shiur* in the intervening weeks. After Reb Leizer lectured a short while, Reb Yisrael had no trouble turning the *shiurim* over to him altogether. The students saw his genius.

Reb Leizer Gordon married the daughter of Avraham Yitzchak Neveizer, a Torah scholar who was also the chief financial backer of Reb Yisrael's yeshiva in Kovno. As long as Reb Leizer could continue his studies, assured as he was of the financial support of his father-in-law, he refused offers of prestigious rabbinic posts. When his father-in-law died, Reb Leizer replaced him as halachic decisor (*moreh tzedek*) in Vilna (a position Avraham Yitzchak Neveizer had filled without pay).

Three months later, Reb Leizer Gordon was appointed rabbi of Kelm. It was 1874, and Reb Leizer was 33. Not in recent memory had someone this young occupied this rabbinate, but Reb Leizer's manner and erudition quickly established his authority.

He served in Kelm ten years, then one-half year in Slobodka, and then: Telshe.

Here, his reputation as an incisive Talmudic lecturer attracted talented students. From the very beginning, his rabbinate in Telshe became synonymous with his rank as *rosh yeshiva*.

Rarely has a yeshiva established itself as a major Torah center as quickly as Telshe. This was due to Reb Leizer Gordon's intellectual charisma; to his curricular shift from the fine-point *pilpul* of some *acharonim* to the incisive analysis of *rishonim* and of *Ketzos HaChoshen*; to his employment (later) of his son-in-law, Rabbi Yosef Leib Bloch, and of Rabbi Shimon Shkop; and, finally, to his manifest love of his students.

Reb Leizer Gordon's thirst for Talmud study was voracious.

Once, two people approached him to adjudicate a *din Torah* or dispute. He asked them to wait, inasmuch as he was in the midst of handling a communal matter. Then, students of the Telshe yeshiva approached him with a Talmudic query (*kushiyyah*). He immediately entered the fray of sophisticated Talmudic give-and-take, discussing the query (and, presumably, a string of related subjects) for hours.

His litigants watched, dumbfounded. Here, the *rosh yeshiva* had asked them to wait, pleading a time conflict, and now he had dropped everything to talk Talmud!

When he "came to"—when he noticed his litigants' stupefaction—he apologized, explaining that when it came to Torah study, he was akin to an addict. He could no more control himself when he heard words of Torah than a drunk could control himself when he saw wine.

Disarmingly honest, energetic, worldly wise, unable to be bought financially or psychologically, Reb Leizer Gordon protected workers from rapacious employers, rid the marketplace in Telshe of false weights and measures, and gave liberally of his small salary to *tzedakah*.

A number of vivid memoirs record the youthful exuberance of rebellious students in Telshe, including the late, revered Ponovitcher *Rav*, Rabbi Yosef Cahaneman. Try as I can, I cannot ascertain from these memoirs, vivid as they are, the true wellspring of rebellion within Telshe. It seems to have been that Reb Leizer Gordon was, simply, too successful (as it were) in instilling love of Talmudic learning. His students rebelled against fixed times for Musar study since they wished to devote every last minute to Talmud study. Reb Leizer Gordon insisted that Musar study occupy a regular place within the curriculum, and he was willing to go so far as to close the yeshiva were this schedule violated.

It was, and the yeshiva was closed.

This was no ordinary rebellion—on either side. His students, including future *gedolei Torah*, rebelled (it seems) for sheer desire to study Talmud. Reb Leizer Gordon knew that an intellectual-emotional framework for deepening fear of Heaven, and finding one's purpose within Torah study—the framework of Musar study—was indispensable. And so, rather than split into irreconcilable camps, the students kept coming back to the *rosh yeshiva*, pleading for the Telshe yeshiva to reopen; and the *rosh yeshiva* kept finding ways to open it, without compromising his position, by employing the unique trait of love.

Love of Hashem is the pinnacle of the ten lofty traits in Bachya ibn Pakuda's classic Musar work, *Chovos Halevavos, Duties of the Heart*. Love, the highest duty of the heart, is not a word to be used lightly, not a trait to be applied loosely.

In the case of Reb Leizer Gordon, love is the only word.

One night, to protest a strict schedule of Musar study, Telshe students clumsily extinguished oil lamps in the yeshiva, then rushed out amid smoke and fear of fire. Reb Leizer quickly ordered the lamps relit, and the students reassembled.

Out of love for him, they obeyed.

Then he fainted.

And fainted—several times throughout the night.

The students feared for him, went without sleep.

At noon the next day he addressed the student body in a moment of high drama. "You know me," he opened. "I do not easily faint. I am not weak, nor do I fear anyone." When his daughter, the wife of Rabbi Yosef Leib Bloch, recently died—he reminded them—it was he who stood strong, gave comfort to his family, resumed his Talmud lectures the moment the seven-day mourning concluded.

"Last night only, my strength failed me.

"Why?

"Because my daughter's death was my personal tragedy, while what happened last night wounded not just me, but the entire world."

The *rosh yeshiva* went on to describe how local Torah centers (*batei midrash*) were emptying, how youth were abandoning study of Torah, how yeshivas were the last hope—and now, how secret meetings and open rebellion in Telshe were the last straw, the reduction of true Jewish civilization to waste.

Love of Hashem's Torah generally, love of his students specifically, unhinged him more openly than even the death of his daughter.

Did he not love his daughter?

The question is wrong. It was not that he loved his daughter less than his students; it was that he loved his students as much as his daughter. The pains of his private loss he could soothe privately. The pains of his public loss—of loss of Torah study to the world—he could not necessarily soothe, or control, at all.

So from love, he fainted.

And from love, his students returned to their studies.

Parush (Ascetic)

Rabbi Avraham Shenker, born in 1846, holds a unique niche in the history of the Musar movement—a sad niche, and a powerful one.

It is sad because he died young, at 42, far from all familiar spiritual habitation. He came under the influence of Reb Yisrael in the early 1860s when Reb Yisrael visited Kovno. The last three-and-a-half years of his life he spent in Italy, trying unsuccessfully to recover from lung disorders. His friend, Baron Simeon Rothschild of Frankfurt, offered to pay the cost of transport for burial in Kovno. His wife, Sarah, said no.

Avraham and Sarah.

The Shenker household was always open, notwithstanding "Reb Abramchik Tanis' " ascetic temperament.[1] To enable her husband to devote himself to service of G-d (in his case, devotion is precisely the word), Sarah Shenker opened a small restaurant in their home, always playing the hostess.

Devotion.

Wrote Rabbi Dov Katz:

"R. Avraham Shenker's regimen of fasts and ascetic denial had its critics. Once they urged Rabbi Nosson Zvi Finkel [later the Alter of Slobodka] to find a way to break R. Avraham's regimen; and to consider whether to write Reb Yisrael Salanter to have him command R. Avraham to stop. Rabbi Nosson Zvi replied that he, too, opposed a regimen of fasts, but that in order to be R. Avraham, it was worthwhile."

---

1. The "Tanis" in his name had nothing to do with his regimen of fasts. He married the daughter of a distinguished Kovno Jew, Reb Tanchum. The *Tanis* is a shortened form of *Tanchum*, indicating that Rabbi Shenker joined the house of Tanchum.

And so, he fasted; he prayed; he studied; he reached for a level of devotion—of concentrated pulling together of energy within every pore—that admitted of no distraction from the pursuit of purity.

The concentrated spiritual energy had its impact.

Reb Abramchik Tanis was one of the few in the Musar movement who won the unqualified attention of Rabbi Yosef Yozel Hurvitz. Reb Yozel, later the Alter of Novorodock, would turn the pursuit of purity into the largest school of thought and action within the Musar movement. Reb Abramchik Tanis (rabbi in upper Alexot, near Kovno) died alone, almost, in Italy; Rabbi Naftali Amsterdam (rabbi in lower Alexot) died alone, almost, in Jerusalem. Rabbi Naftali had his Reb Aryeh Levin; Reb Abramchik had his Reb Yozel—a powerful legacy. *"Tzaddikim* in their deaths are greater than in their lives."

Concentration.

Devotion.

"He who saw R. Avraham Shenker pray could only respond with such emotion, it was as if the sight could take the place of Musar study" (Rabbi Dov Katz).

This was no metaphor.

It is common to find in the lists of resolutions that *ba'alei Musar* or Musar masters wrote during the days before Rosh Hashanah, Yom Kippur, or Passover, the aspiration "to pray in the Musar way" once a day or once a week.

"Prayer in the Musar way" is the incorporation of Musar study into the recitation of the *Shemoneh Esrei.* It is the intentional, concentrated build-up of emotion, the extraction of every last scintilla of inspiration from a personally chosen line of prayer or verse of *Tanach*, the Hebrew Bible. Musar study, as conceived by Reb Yisrael, is only partially the apprehension of teachings in Musar books. Its other part is the repeated singing, humming, chanting, or even shouting of a single, poignant Biblical verse. It is learning "with lips aflame," in Reb Yisrael's words.

Take *Psalms* 51:12: *"A pure heart create in me, O G-d."*

Or *Psalms* 31:16: *"My times are in Your hand . . ."*

Or *Psalms* 111:10: *"The beginning of wisdom is the fear of Hashem."*

Take any verse that you yourself find moving, said Reb Yisrael. Take it, repeat it. Once, twice, one-hundred times, five-hundred times.

A message *penetrates.*

Deep into the self.

Purity becomes not a word, but a reality. Faith—the Divine presence in all times—becomes not a concept, but an experience. *Yir'as Hashem* becomes not an abstraction, but a moving force.

In "prayer in the Musar way," a line of prayer triggers, by association, a line of *Tanach* that one repeats over and over, infusing one's entire *Shemoneh Esrei* with an intensity and intention that commands—compels—one to face His presence. Or, quite simply, a line of prayer itself is repeated, over and over, transporting one to a separate, higher spiritual dimension: *"Purify our hearts to serve You in truth"*; *"Return us in perfect repentance before You."*

Repeated.

Over and over.

A message *penetrates.*

Prayer in the Musar way adds time—duration—to prayer, and transforms the person who prays into a visible object of awe, a swaying vessel, as it were, of the Divine light.

I know what they meant when they spoke of Reb Abramchik Tanis' prayer as a searing stimulant of Musar consciousness because I have witnessed in prayer Reb Leib Friedman, a *ba'al Musar* in whom this Musar technique—prayer in the Musar way—remains a living method. An absolutely self-effacing, utterly retiring, hidden seeker in Jerusalem, Reb Leib Friedman in his prayer—his rhythmic grasping of worlds that seems so beyond anything I think I have ever known—calls to my mind the type of visage that those who witnessed Reb Abramchik Tanis must have responded to.

I can therefore understand why Reb Abramchik Tanis left his imprint on the greatest of Reb Yisrael's disciples. I can understand why the Alter of Slobodka said: Do not touch him. Let him be. I can understand why Rabbi Naftali Amsterdam considered him his friend, why Reb Itzele Peterburger welcomed his active participation in the Kovno *Kolel*, and why the Alter of Novorodock drew so much sustenance from him. I can understand the fortitude and the faith that must have guided Reb Abramchik Tanis in his last, lonely years; and, possibly, why his wife wished to let him be, in Italy, in his final resting. Those final years of prayer, in that place—I imagine—must have transformed that place, invested it, so to speak, with a devotion, a *kedushah*, that penetrated it.

That irradiated it.

There, he was fit to rest.

Lay Leader

Where to start? To say that Rabbi Eliyahu Levinsohn was thoroughly conversant in the entire Talmud? That he was a wealthy banker, and immensely generous? That he resolved disputes, pulled to peaceful relations recalcitrant opponents? That he risked his livelihood to defy his employer when public welfare was at stake? That he stood firmly before the Tsar's minions, yet withdrew into a shell when others wished to acknowledge his greatness?

Born in 1822, in Kartinga, Lithuania, Eliyahu Levinsohn came to Salant in about 1830 with the reputation as an *illui*. Reb Yisrael, then about 20, took the eight-year-old prodigy under his wing, taught him much of theTalmud over the next three years, and impressed upon him the regimen and rewards of Musar.

When he was only 12, Rabbi Elinka Kartinger (as he came to be called) demonstrated a talent for arbitrating financial disputes. Talmudic acumen, common sense, and arithmetical wizardry attracted many to his services.

Rabbi Elinka received enticing offers to serve in important rabbinic posts. Reb Yisrael believed that a different task best suited his talents. Accordingly, Rabbi Elinka took over his (deceased) father's business, had good success, and was asked to direct a large bank in Kovno.

One of the bank's largest clients went bankrupt, and the bank lost 100,000 rubles. Rabbi Elinka considered himself responsible for the loss even though the owner of the bank did not), resigned his position, opened his own business, and, without being asked, repaid the 100,000 rubles.

Musar!

And a good name: investors knew that Rabbi Elinka was completely trustworthy; his various businesses, investments, and banks flourished internationally.

Throughout, Rabbi Elinka resided in the *shtetl* of his birth, Kartinga. Of course, he had to travel, but most of the time he lived in his small, quiet hamlet, conducive to intensive Torah study. He retained the thirst for the Torah study of his youth—the thirst, and the talent.

Business.

Torah study.

And: public service. Rabbi Elinka headed the *Kolel Vilna—Zamot* for 40 years, concerning himself with the needs of Jews in *Eretz Yisrael*. He played an active role in coordinating the presentation of Jewish concerns to Russian Tsars, weaving his way through the corridors of power in St. Petersburg. He financed Reb Yisrael's efforts in establishing *batei Musar*. He supported Torah students with monthly stipends, dispensed *tzedakah* to countless needy, and provided dowries to brides.

Rabbi Dov Katz (based on Yaakov Mark) described Rabbi Elinka's household in Kartinga:

"Jews and Gentiles from all over the Zamot region of Lithuania entered his house at all hours of the day—one person with a commercial transaction, one in need of a loan, another in need of advice, still another with a communal issue, someone with a request for charity, and someone else with a request for a recommendation. In the midst of all this a rabbi from one of the nearby towns would suddenly appear to take counsel on a serious halachic question for which he would not take sole responsibility."

In all this there was a certain tone, a Musar tone.

Kindliness. Once a person was seen following Rabbi Elinka to his house. When Rabbi Elinka entered, the person slipped into the kitchen and made inquiries. The following unfolded: This person, a sailor unemployed for two years, had secured work only the day before as chief of supplies for a ship about to set sail. He was given 150 rubles to buy the necessary supplies. Then the money was stolen from him in the marketplace. He contemplated drowning himself, but an unknown young gentleman—Rabbi Elinka—appeared from out of nowhere and asked why he appeared depressed. He told his story and before he knew what happened Rabbi Elinka had given him 150 rubles. The sailor asked his name, in order to repay the debt, but Rabbi Elinka refused. "When you become wealthy," he said, "you help someone yourself."

Courtesy. Rabbi Elinka was called "a living *Shulchan Aruch.*" Like Reb Yisrael, Rabbi Elinka exerted himself for *hiddur mitzvah*—mitzvah performance in the most exemplary way—but never at someone else's expense. In a conflict between even ordinary performance of a *mitzvah* and human needs, he would opt to meet the human needs, and to perform the *mitzvah* in a less than ordinary, minimal fashion. For example, he would pray *ma'ariv* earlier than the usual time in order to prevent his household help from waiting for him and getting hungry.

Courage. Tsarist authorities in St. Petersburg sporadically summoned a committee of rabbis and layman for advice on Jewish affairs. The owner of the bank which Rabbi Elinka administered desired to be elected to the committee. Rabbi Elinka, knowing his employer's ideological inclinations not to be in accord with the Torah, traveled to Vilna to campaign agains this election, and in fact he was not elected.

He was, understandably, furious.

Rabbi Elinka's position was endangered.

He told his employer that his opposition was nothing personal, that his first loyalty had to be to his G-d and his people. There had to be something deeply sincere in Rabbi Elinka's appeal, for not only was he not fired, he was promoted.

Concealment. Rabbi Elinka once sought advice from Rabbi Dr. Ezriel Hildesheimer (head of the Orthodox rabbinical seminary in Berlin), introducing himself as "Levinsohn." When Rabbi Elinka was about to leave, Rabbi Hildesheimer asked whether he lived close to Kartinga, and whether he knew "Rabbi Elinka Kartinga." Rabbi Elinka thought a bit, then said that he knew someone named Eliyahu Levinsohn, who was mistakenly called "Rabbi Elinka Kartinga." Rabbi Hildesheimer became angry, criticizing his guest for making light of a great person, and then extending his criticism to Russian Jews generally, for not recognizing their national greats.

Sudden recoil.

Rabbi Hildesheimer changed his tune, and tone: "Perhaps my distinguished guest is Rabbi Elinka?!"

Of course, he was.

In his last will and testament, Rabbi Elinka requested that when the End approached his door, ten students of Torah stand next to his bed, recite *mishnayos* from *Kodoshim* and *Taharos*, and that one of the students call out: "Perhaps the Lord of Hosts will be gracious to Rabbi Elinka, such that his mind will be clear, that he may depart from this world amidst words of Torah."

At his funeral, in 1888, Rabbi Alexander Moshe Lapidos, a childhood friend and fellow disciple of Reb Yisrael, said:

> Were the generation worthy, were the Holy One, Blessed be He, to awaken the hearts and minds of the rulers of the nations, to gather in the dispersed of Israel, and then to choose a national leader, a spokesman for all the people—the greatest in the generation, always alert, acceptable to all factions, a man of peace—who could better qualify as the Divine representative (*nesi Elohim*) than Rabbi Elinka?"

Maggid (Preacher)

Where to start? To say that "the *Maggid* of Kelm"—Rabbi Moshe Yitzchak Darshan—was a crusader for justice? That he sacrificed his job to rescue widows and orphans from an unscrupulous financial planner? That he founded tens of *batei Musar*? That he had a foreboding of the Holocaust? That he could set before an audience a picture of truth, of Divine punishment, and of Divine reward, so powerfully, so lucidly, that the emotions rose to the surface, with weeping overcoming his listeners—and himself?

The *Maggid* of Kelm brought new respect to an old and somewhat discredited profession, that of traveling preacher. He came to Reb Yisrael in Kovno in the 1850s with a promising career in *maggidus* off track. Unlike many *maggidim*, who were well-meaning ne'er-do-wells, Rabbi Moshe Yitzchak Darshan had a quick mind and good training in Talmud. In fact, his career as a *maggid* had failed because his sermons were too philosophical and abstract. Born in 1828, he came to Reb Yisrael in his mid-twenties, looking for direction.

Just as Reb Yisrael's innovative turn of mind identified a new need to undertake a formal program for training *rashei yeshiva* (yeshiva deans), so, too, his fresh perspective perceived new potential in *maggidus*. Then practiced in Lithuania mainly by poverty stricken ex-teachers, the profession offered the opportunity to influence the mass of common householders—if the right candidate could be found.

Before coming to Vilna as a yeshiva dean, Reb Yisrael himself had considered becoming a *maggid*, rejecting it as unsuitable only for himself, but not in principle. And so, it made eminent sense that when a suitable candidate presented himself, "when Rabbi Moshe Yitzchak arrived in Kovno, he immediately attracted the attention of Reb Yisrael, who was taken aback by his true fear of Heaven, and by his enormous talent to influence others" (Yaakov Mark).

Rabbi Moshe Yitzchak did not remain in Kovno long.

It seems that he needed only the confidence to be gained from an authoritative evaluation of his talents, and of their potential for enriching the deeds and character of others. All this Reb Yisrael gave him so powerfully, so lucidly, that the future *Maggid* of Kelm would leave his imprint across the small towns of Lithuania for the next half-century. Reb Yisrael gave him something else, too: a way to make his message more popular and pertinent—an understanding of the centrality of the ethical side of Halachah.

The *Maggid* of Kelm became known for his passionate attachment to justice and honesty.

Example:

He stimulated "pogroms" (as Rabbi Dov Katz put it) in the marketplace. He preached so effectively against false weights and measures—against lying and cheating in business—that storekeepers were moved to action. He preached that as shopkeepers practiced "service of G-d," they practiced "service of the store." Their zealous "service of the store" made them lie and cheat. "With the same yearning and enthusiasm that one brings to service of Hashem, one brings to service of the store," wrote the *Maggid*. Quite simply: Cheaters were idolotors.

The message worked: Marketplaces were overturned. Shopkeepersdestroyed false scales and measures. Then they made their way to the *Maggid* for instructions in *teshuvah* . . .

Example:

In Kelm there was a strong trade in Prussian salt, which came in two types: white and red. The red salt was the higher quality. Two Jewish traders mixed a red dye with the white salt to produce a fraudulent red salt, which commanded a higher price. From the pulpit the *Maggid* of Kelm denounced the "salt of Sodom" (that is, salt produced with the deceitful ways of Sodom) and castigated the fraudulent traders by name.

It didn't help.

The *Maggid* threatened to stand outside the trading stalls to inform customers that the red salt was really white.

The traders denounced the *Maggid* to the police. For having the courage of his convictions—of the Torah's convictions—he went to jail.

But not for long.

A order came from higher-ups to free the *Maggid*.

It seems that the regional postmaster revered the *Maggid* for his honesty. The postmaster had observed the *Maggid* on more than one occasion tear up stamps, and asked why. The *Maggid* replied that whenever he sent a letter by private messenger, he tore a stamp so as not to deprive the State of the income that was rightfully its own.

When word got around of the *Maggid*'s arrest, the postmaster put in the good word to free him.

It is heartening when might takes the side of right, but it did not always work this way for the *Maggid*, who then defied might for the sake of right. In his third year in Kelm, he publicly denounced financial planners who represented themselves to widows and orphans as responsible investors.

They were not.

The *Maggid*'s warning enabled the poor to withdraw from shaky schemes, but also cost him his job.

"*Maggid* of Kelm" stuck as Rabbi Moshe Yitzchak's name even though he was in Kelm only three years. In fact, the *Maggid* preferred the life of the wanderer. Like many of the famous personalities in the Musar movement, who were either orphaned or left home young, the *Maggid* was orphaned at the age of ten. Under that stern compression of circumstance, a person can wither, or muster a unique inner fortitude and independence of spirit. The familiar trappings of a home and a native city never seemed to be strong needs of the *Maggid*. He was satisfied to do the work of Hashem. He transcended the common comforts of home and familiar surroundings.

He was born near Slonim, then went to Slonim when his father died. He was an outstanding Talmud student there, married at the age of 18, then went into business elsewhere. He returned to Slonim when his business failed, and became a *maggid* in Slonim. His fearless denunciations of dishonesty compelled him to leave for another town. Here, he was "discovered" by the rabbi of Iviyah, who appreciated his potential and advised him to change his orientation from philosophy to practical Halachah. To do that, the *Maggid* went to study under Reb Yisrael Salanter.

Following his decisive molding by Reb Yisrael, the *Maggid* began to wander across Lithuania, honing his skills as a preacher and founding alarge number of *batei Musar*. In his travels, he came to Kelm. There, he was so well liked that he was hired as the "*Maggid* of Kelm"—and the name stuck. The name—and the reputation.

His Talmud learning attracted *lamdanim* (rabbinical scholars); his earnestness attracted common folk; his attacks attracted the attention of *maskilim* or secular enlighteners. His fearlessness attracted all of them because it was toward all that his admonitions were directed. The storekeeper with honest weights and measures—he would say—will claim a greater portion in the world-to-come than some rabbis. The dishonest storekeeper with fraudulent weights and measures—he would say—will earn special torments in Gehenna. The unbelieving *maskil*—he would say—will suffer likewise.

But he wouldn't just "say." He would build transparent parables; everyone would know whom he was criticizing. He would sing, he would cry, he would cite Talmud and Midrash and Bible; he would stand four to five hours until he was drenched in sweat—until his audience was moved to tears and to action, or to opposition.

Either way, the message penetrated.

For a simple reason.

As a *ba'al Musar*, he was interested in cultivating truth, whatever its source, and in criticizing sin, whatever its nature—sin against Hashem or sin against man.

A perceiver of sin, a knower of evil, an analyzer of power and deception, he peered into the refined German nation—to which *maskilim* urged young Jews to betake themselves, to replace commitment to *mitzvos* with "culture" and "refinement"—the *Maggid* peered deeply. During the Franco-German war, this is what he saw, and said:

> The German will not persecute the Jews in an ordinary way. He will not be a simple assailant. . . . Rather, he will turn anti-Semitism into a systematic altar (*shulchan aruch*), Heaven rescue us . . . There will arise a new *Shulchan Aruch*—a German Code of Law—against the Jewish people, and therein, Heaven rescue us, it will be written: "The best of the Jews, kill! The best of the Jews, kill!"

Jews listened to the *Maggid* of Kelm, whether they liked his message or not, because they knew he spoke the truth.

Patron of Musar

Rabbi Binyamin Zilber once stressed to me:
"We must always remember: poverty is also a great *nisayon* (trial)."

Also?

Is not poverty a greater trial than wealth?

"*Sefarim* emphasize that the greatest test is wealth," Rabbi Binyamin answered me, "but this should not desensitize us to the pains of poverty."

Wealth is the greater trial because it imposes a severe responsibility for the poor—for the doing of righteous deeds—and because it can divert attention from *avodas Hashem*—from becoming a righteous person.

Shraga Feivel Frank, born in about 1843, died at the age of 43, bequeathing an incomparable will to create a legacy of Torah and Musar. His posthumous will created a uniquely fertile dedication in Eastern Europe, Israel, and America—but more on this below. It can be understood only by setting forth Shraga Feivel Frank's dedication in life.

His life is the story of great success in business as the owner of a tannery. But there is a larger story still—the story of what he achieved with his wealth, for himself and for others.

He not only performed righteous deeds, he became a righteous person.

When he died, no eulogy or eulogist was needed to bring the Jews in Kovno to mourning. "*Reb Shraga Feivel died*": these words alone—nothing more—reduced citizens of Kovno to tears. His deeds and demeanor had made him beloved.

Here are Reb Shraga Feivel Frank's righteous deeds—what he did for others:

◀§ Reb Shraga Feivel built a very large home, but only about a third of it was for him and his family.

A whole floor was for guests.

The attic was for Torah scholars. Reb Yisrael Salanter studied there for days at a time. It was his *beis hisbodedus* in the Kovno area. It was also his *beis hamidrash* for private instruction and impassioned *Musar shmuesn* for his most capable disciples. Many of the Musar teachings that originated with Reb Yisrael originated in the home of Reb Shraga Feivel Frank.

As if this were not enough, Reb Shraga Feivel's home was a nerve center for Torah and Musar when Reb Yisrael was away, in Western Europe. Reb Shraga Feivel's home was used as a *beis hamidrash* and *beis hamusar* by the Alter of Kelm, Rabbi Naftali Amsterdam, Reb Abramchik Tanis, the Chafetz Chaim, the Alter of Slobodka, the Alter of Novorodock, and other luminaries, such as Rabbi Alexander Moshe Lapidus, disciple of Reb Yisrael and communal rabbi of Rassein for 40 years. Reb Itzele Peterburger's 40 days in *hisbodedus* between *rosh chodesh Elul* and Yom Kippur were usually spent in Reb Shraga Feivel's attic.

Reb Shraga Feivel himself underwrote a *kolel*—the seed of the Kovno *Kolel* founded by Reb Yisrael Salanter and Rabbi Yitzchak Elchanan Spektor—in his own home. Rabbi Isser Zalman Meltzer once remarked that Reb Shraga Feivel supported all the yeshivas of Slobodka.

❧ *"Zerizim makdimim lamitzvos"*: zealots in the service of Hashem do His work at the earliest possible opportunity.

Upon returning from work every evening, Reb Shraga Feivel Frank balanced his books, calculated his profit for the day, and separated a tenth of the profits for *tzedakah* on the spot.

Sometimes, the *tzedakah* was not money. A Torah scholar, ascending to the Land of Israel and taking his leave of Reb Shraga Feivel, suddenly found himself presented with Reb Shraga Feivel's winter fur coat. The scholar refused to accept, but Reb Shraga Feivel successfully insisted, pointing out that in sailing to Israel, and living in Jerusalem or Safed, the scholar would need the coat more than someone in Kovno.

Whenever possible, Reb Shraga Feivel hid his acts of *tzedakah*.

When he heard of Torah scholars unable to feed their families, he filled his wagon with foodstuffs and delivered them personally, in the middle of the night, when all were sleeping. "Great is he who performs *tzedakah* secretly" (*Bava Basra* 9b).

✦§ Once, a Torah scholar, a competitor of Reb Shraga Feivel, was on the verge of bankruptcy. The failed tannery owner's reneging on commitments could lead to a scandal, a *chillul Hashem*. Reb Shraga Feivel gave him a very large sum to reestablish his business on a firm footing.

Here, he helped his competitor.

He also helped his tenants.

Reb Shraga Feivel built housing for some of his factory workers. He made it a point to learn when a worker would be unable to pay the a month's rent, when, say, his wife had just given birth. Reb Shraga Feivel would advance the rent to his worker, who would then be able to avoid the embarrassment of begging for a reprieve from the rent collector. Likewise, Reb Shraga Feivel would be able to avoid telling his collector to skip a certain address, and thus, too, avoid embarrassing the worker before the collector.

Here is Reb Shraga Feivel's righteousness—what he did to nurture his own piety:

✦§ The Alter of Slobodka once related that he sat at Reb Shraga Feivel's Frank's table, together with several Torah scholars and other important people. Reb Shraga Feivel wished to serve his guests, so he rang for the servants.

The servants did not come.

The conversation continued for several minutes. Reb Shraga Feivel rang again.

The servants did not come.

So it went, several times.

The guests wondered out loud: Why is there not more discipline in this household? Said Reb Shraga Feivel:

"I have great joy now. All my days I wonder, in regard to my servants, whether I violate the Torah's injunction: *'Over your brehren, the children of Israel, do not rule oppressively, one over another'* (*Leviticus* 25:46). When I see that my servants have no fear of me, I take comfort."

When house guests arrived in the Frank home, Reb Shraga Feivel himself, and his daughters, would prepare the beds—not the servants. When large numbers of guests arrived, and there were not enough beds, the doors were removed from the hinges, and the Frank girls slept on them—not the servants. The Frank girls used to serve the guests—not the servants.

It was not only that righteous deeds were to be done for others—for guests—but also that righteousness was to be embodied personally. Reb Shraga Feivel's wealth did not blind him to that obligation, not for himself—and not for his family:

When the Frank daughters went to buy clothing, their father told them that they could buy the best, but that afterwards, they could not flaunt what they had bought.

Once a stranger entered Reb Shraga Feivel's factory, and asked for a discount on a large quantity of leather. Reb Shraga Feivel replied that he never bargained, that he built a certain profit margin into his pricing, and that if his inquirer chose, he could shop elsewhere. To facilitate that, Reb Shraga Feivel supplied him with several addresses.

The merchant shopped elsewhere, found that Reb Shraga Feivel's prices were the best, and returned to his tannery to pay the asking price, only to be greeted with this pronouncement: "I'll sell you the the leather at the discount you asked for."

To the merchant's astonishment, Reb Shraga Feivel explained:

"When you left, I considered. You desired to buy such a large quantity that I really could discount it and still be left with sufficient profit. Now that you've returned and offered to pay the original, higher price, I must stand by what I decided, as King David taught in *Psalms* (15:1-2): 'Who shall live in Your Tent? Who shall dwell on Your holy mountain? He who walks with integrity, does righteousness, *and speaks the truth in his heart.'*

" 'To speak the truth in the heart': this is to stand by one's word, not only when it is uttered, but even when it is thought, as Rashi (*Makkos* 24a) recorded of Rav Safra:

" 'Rav Safra wished to sell a certain item. A buyer approached him when he was reciting *Shema* and said, *Sell it to me at such-and-such a price.* Rav Safra did not respond since he was in the middle of *Shema*. The buyer figured that Rav Safra was holding out for a higher price, and the buyer offered one. When Rav Safra finished *Shema*, he said, *Give me the price you mentioned originally, for I decided to sell to you when you stated your price originally.*' "

If Reb Shraga Feivel's wealth was a condition to be enjoyed, but not flaunted—not before others, not before himself—neither was it to be acquired by fraud, even against his own mental commitments. His personal integrity was at the root of both his righteousness—his own sense of serving Hashem—and of his righteous deeds, his service of Hashem's creatures.

Often, his personal piety and ethical deeds interpenetrated each other. Once, a man asked Reb Shraga Feivel for a substantial loan. Reb Shraga Feivel assented. The time for repayment came and went. In accord with his custom, Reb Shraga Feivel did not seek out the borrower.

More time passed, and Reb Shraga Feivel himself needed a loan. Mrs. Golda Frank, his wife, remembered the unpaid debt, and went to the borrower to ask for it. Able to repay, the borrower brazenly refused to do so.

Still more time passed, and behold! The borrower appeared to request a second loan. He would repay it, he said, together with the first obligation.

Stunned at the audacity, Reb Shraga Feivel asked for time to think. His wife said plainly: He probably will not repay either loan. Reb Shraga Feivel considered, then said:

Dear Golda, are we any better than he? Every high holy day season, we beseech the Holy One, Blessed be He, for forgiveness for all our sins. When we stand there, seeking forgiveness, obligating ourselves to perfect repentance, we mean it with all our hearts. We say it every year, yet we fall back into our old ways, every year.

Now this Jew, at this moment, means it with all his heart when he promises to repay the new loan, and the old loan. Hashem, looking at us, seeing our failure to live up to our own obligations, is merciful. Must we not be merciful to this Jew?

Golda and Shraga Feivel Frank extended the loan.

"Reb Shraga Feivel died." All of Kovno mourned, not least, of course, his family.

Golda Frank was left with one son, four daughters, and her husband's death-bed request to marry all four daughters to the choicest, budding *talmidei chachamim* or Talmud scholars in the generation.

Here was Reb Shraga Feivel's incomparable will to create a Torah legacy.

It was a will born not of sheer desire, but of a lifetime of achievement in piety and *tzedakah*. It was a will whose seedbed was a life of dedication. It was the kind of will that comes to fruition because of the kind of person who sustained it, and because of the *middos* or pious character traits of the family who nurtured it alongside him.

The Frank's oldest daughter, Chaya Menuchah, married Rabbi Moshe Mordechai Epstein, destined to lead the Slobodka yeshiva in Slobodka, Chevron, and Jerusalem, for 40 years.

The Frank's second daughter, Bayla Hinda, married Rabbi Isser Zalman Meltzer, destined to stand as a symbol of the highest level of Talmud scholarship in Slobodka, Slutz, and Jerusalem, for 60 years.

The Frank's third daughter, Pesha, married Rabbi Baruch Yehoshua Horowitz, Rabbi Naftali Amsterdam's replacement as rabbi of Alexot, and *maggid shiur* or Talmud lecturer in Slobodka, over a span of 36 years.

The Frank's fourth daughter, Devorah, married Rabbi Sheftel Cramer, *mashgiach* in Slutsk, and the founder of one of the first yeshivas in America, in Cleveland, in 1925, even as his sons-in-law, including Rabbi Yitzchak Yaakov Ruderman, founded Ner Israel in Baltimore.

Reb Shraga Feivel Frank: a disciple of Reb Yisrael who met the trials of wealth successfully, who inspirited a will to create an incomparable legacy of Torah and Musar accordingly.

Part Four:
Novorodock and Slobodka Musar

Introduction

Novorodock Musar was loud; Slobodka Musar, quiet. Novorodock was aggressive, Slobodka restrained. Novorodock was interested in quantity—saving the world; Slobodka, in quality—raising up a select group of disciples. Novorodock sought youngsters and teenagers; Slobodka sought somewhat older, budding scholars. Novorodock was outwardly emotional, Slobodka inwardly so. Novorodock was spontaneous; Slobodka, polished.

In one sense, Novorodock's horizons were wide, producing activists willing to go anywhere to disseminate Torah and Musar; in another sense, Novorodock was concentrated, explicitly, defiantly, and utterly negating all studies and pursuits outside of Torah.

In one sense, Slobodka's horizons were wide, viewing certain realities outside of Torah—styles of dress, for example—as valuable for winning its respect. In another sense, Slobodka was concentrated, producing an elite of thinkers and scholars.

Novorodock and Slobodka, different though they were, shared more than is commonly realized. Both were led by *parushim:* as the Alter of Novorodock separated from family for long periods, so did the Alter of Slobodka. Both Novorodock and Slobodka stressed the importance of man's inner state, regarding its purification as essential to true service of Hashem.

Both Novorodock and Slobodka differed from Kelm Musar.

Kelm trusted slow, gradual progress in *avodas Hashem*, while Novorodock and Slobodka trusted bold, dramatic advances. Kelm said that Novorodock and Slobodka had to have very special seekers — *yechidei segullah* — to advance rapidly, boldly. Novorodock and Slobodka replied that Kelm had to have very special seekers to complete the painstakingly gradual, thorough training in Kelm.

Novorodock and Slobodka, alike though they were, differed in ways not commonly realized. Novorodock, "negating the world," produced resilient, joyous personalities with a distinct earthiness— the earthiness springing from knowledge of unworthy desires to be overcome. Slobodka, stressing "the greatness of man," produced delicate, refined personalities, noble in their luminous piety—a luminosity born of having utterly removed themselves from, rather than worked through, unworthy desires. Novorodock dug deep, into depths of human evil, in order to transcend; Slobodka looked upward, past evil, in order to ascend. The Alter of Novorodock said: "What you cannot do, you must do." The Alter of Slobodka said: "What you cannot do, you must rise above."

8.

Novorodock Musar

ovorodock Musar: *laughter?*
Yes, laughter.
Even when I studied with him years ago, Rabbi
Yitzchak Orlansky was one of the last, and the oldest,
of the living disciples of the Alter of Novorodock,
Rabbi Yosef Yozel Hurvitz.

We studied weekly.

We studied serious matters. *Bitachon*. Self-criticism. The power of the self to withstand embarrassment, even to grow from it. Asceticism, self-denial. Even: slave labor in Siberia, and Nazism, lost relatives and communities, all murdered.

Serious matters.

But every time I left Rabbi Orlansky's home, I had something of a stomach ache.

And a good deal of wonder about the strength of his chairs.

Every time I learned with Rabbi Orlansky, he had me laughing. Laughing so hard that I inevitably bounced up and down on his chair.

He was not telling jokes.

Rabbi Orlansky was no comedian.

He is a Musarnik, a person who takes his life and his tasks with utmost seriousness.

No, not jokes, just an infectious love of life, an inner and utter freedom from life's temptations and taxations, a freedom so pervasive that life's absurdities merely toss themselves up to Rabbi Orlansky, such that simple, warm, infectious laughter—smiles and grins and laughs—are the only possible response.

When one is not tied to vexations of life, one can derive a most natural and pervasive enjoyment from observing its tenacles. It is not a question of poking fun—this is alien to Rabbi Orlansky—it is a question of taking pleasure from everything that happens.

It is a question of being so deeply imbued with life as the Divine creation—with each breath, each flash of color, each fragrance and intellectual formulation, each event—that pleasure and love, even of life's absurdities, are the only possible response.

And so Rabbi Orlansky, from his perch of perfection (if there be such a thing), from his lifetime of learning to transform every emotion, thought, and gesture under the sanctity of the ways of Hashem—the commandments of Torah—looked at life, and laughed.

A laughter of enjoyment, not derision.

Of love, not scorn.

Of pleasure, not pain.

Occasionally Rabbi Orlansky experienced lapse of memory. We have ominous names for this today. We have signs, verbal and non-verbal, to connote tragedy when we speak of this.

For Rabbi Orlansky, lapse of memory was nothing but one more wondrous and life-inspiriting development that befell the human being.

He would repeat something to me. Then he would pause, look about, open and close those happy eyes of his, so creased from smiling, and blurt out in that childlike way of his:

"Wait! Didn't I just say that a moment ago?" He would look about, smile, absorb the light and the shadow from wherever they impinged, and say to this effect: "How mysterious the workings of the mind. I just said something, and now I forgot it! How *wondrous* the workings of the mind! Aha!"

Decay and knowledge, color and shape, suffering and *simchah*: every imaginable occurance generated for Rabbi Orlansky a heightened sense of wonder.

This he took from Novorodock Musar.

People who only read about Novorodock often draw conclusions opposed to its spirit. Novorodock Musar, especially, is not given to armchair understanding. To be fully understood, it must be practiced.

People who have submerged themselves in the Novorodock reality know that its living essence is the spirit of Rabbi Orlansky.

They know that there is no freer and happier individual than a Novorodock Musarnik.

They know that the clarity and unself-consciousness of Rabbi Eliezer Ben Zion Bruk, the balance and trust of Rabbi Yehudah Leib Nekritz, the joy and acceptance of Rabbi Yitzchak Orlansky, are the rule, not the exception.

They know that Novorodock Musar is life and love and inner joy.

They know that all this began with the radical Musar experiments of Rabbi Yosef Yozel Hurvitz, the Alter of Novorodock.

The Alter of Novorodock, "Reb Yozel": a legend, and a quandary. Hard to figure out. Hard to understand. A man who retired to the forests, for years. A man who periodically left his wife to study Torah and Musar, and who, after she died in childbirth, locked himself in a cabin for a year-and-a-half, to study Torah and Musar. Reb Yozel, a man beyond the common understanding, beyond the common methods of seeking holiness and happiness. A man who left this world in order to acquire it.

What does this mean, *who left this world in order to acquire it?*

The point comes clear in contrasting Reb Yozel with his mentor, Reb Abramchik Tanis, the ascetic.

On the one hand, Reb Yozel was deeply indebted to Reb Abramchik Tanis. In him Reb Yozel witnessed great discipline at ascetic denial. He witnessed great desire for purity and holiness. He received great encouragement for his own aspirations in *perishus* or separation. And yet, in a certain basic way, Reb Yozel's aspirations diverged from Reb Abramchik Tanis'. Though Reb Yozel denied himself food or housing or other necessities for long stretches, he was not an ascetic. Reb Yozel rejected this world and all of its amenities not as a goal, but as a technique. To Reb Yozel, asceticism was not an end, it was a means.

A means to freedom.

Consider: a person *needs* tasty food, *needs* a fine home, *needs* a fine car or coat. Is this person free? Reb Yozel would say that he is enslaved, that, *needing* as he does all of these trappings of life, he really does not possess them. *They* possess *him*. He owns them, but, in essence, gains no pleasure from them. Since he *needs* them, he cannot live happily without them. And even when he has them, his happiness is impermanent.

It is impermanent not simply because it will fade if his fortunes fade, and he loses ownership over his objects. His happiness is impermanent because it is not self-validating, not rooted *in himself*. It is rooted in objects, and therefore his happiness is subject to an infinite flux. *Anything* can affect it, can spoil it, since it is only superficial, rooted in something outside himself, rather than in himself.

Reb Yozel's Musar search was for happiness, *permanent* happiness—a happiness that could derive pleasure from life regardless of external circumstance. Reb Yozel was a man *of this world*. He wished to enjoy life both when circumstances presented him with nothing—circumstances such as war and hunger—and when circumstances presented him with everything—fine clothing or a fine dwelling.

There was only one way to achieve a permanent sense of pleasure within this world, Reb Yozel learned through his Musar experiments. There was only one way: to negate the world, to separate from it, to free oneself of materialistic desire—of *needs*. Novorodock Musar called this *bittul hayesh*: the world means nothing.

And when the world means nothing, life can mean everything.

When the world and its enticements no longer tug at one's soul, one can love from out of a sheer sense of love, not from a need *to* love or *for* love. One can be pure, can love man and Hashem because they are to be loved; one can serve man and Hashem because they are to be served—for this, and for no other reason.

Reb Yozel wished to be pure not to escape from this world, but to live buoyantly and joyously—above all, freely—within it.

All this is what Reb Yozel wished.

It is one thing to have a wish, quite something else to make it happen.

Reb Yozel made it happen with a lifetime of supreme effort, of supreme discipline, and of *bitachon*.

Yosef Yozel Hurvitz was born in Plungien, a small town in Lithuania, in about 1850. His father, Rabbi Shlomo Zalman Hurvitz, steeped himself in Torah study; his mother supplemented her husband's meagre salary as a *dayyan* or rabbinical judge.

Rabbi Shlomo Zalman Hurvitz was an ascetic, assiduous scholar. He took no interest in financial matters. Hashem and the study of His word—this was his life, and the life he wished for his children.

His son, Yosef Yozel, was bold, fearless, independent. As a child he leapt on untended, harnessed wagons belonging to his father's visitors, and drove them in the nearby forest. Yosef Yozel's father wished to turn this youthful vitality to Talmud study, and he did. Already by the age of 16, Reb Yosef Yozel was delivering lectures in Talmud. But his life was to be jolted by a series of events that turned his vitality away from intensive Talmud study. Only later did great Musar masters, including Reb Yisrael Salanter, show him that his innate qualities could be transformed into fruitful talents in disseminating Torah and Musar. Even under expert guidance, however, Reb Yozel's inner struggles were intense and painful. He ultimately came to justify the sacred use of his qualities through an introspective solitude of the alone before the Alone.

He was, then, at 16, a budding scholar, and at 18, a groom, promised a large dowry, when the first jolt struck. Before his wedding, his prospective father-in-law died. The dowry vanished. Rabbi Shlomo Zalman Hurvitz insisted on honoring the marriage arrangement. Reb Yozel now had to support not only his wife, and not only his mother-in-law, but her eight children! His budding career in Talmudic scholarship was derailed.

With characteristic daring and intelligence, he operated a textile trade, and turned a handsome profit. He acquired expertise, and a reputation for reliability. He traveled extensively between Lithuania and Prussia. His Talmudic studies were now pursued part time—several hours daily, but still, part time.

So it went for several years. Reb Yozel was a learned layman, a good businessman. Then came the second jolt, a message from Reb Yisrael Salanter: perhaps Reb Yozel could, and should, be a scholar after all.

On a business trip in about 1877, Reb Yozel encountered Reb Yisrael in Memel, Prussia.

Reb Yisrael beheld this energetic businessman. He saw below the surface: here was no ordinary merchant. Here was a potential jewel of Torah and Musar. Reb Yisrael pressed him as to why he did not balance his business with more Talmud study. Reb Yozel answered that he had to support 11 souls, including, by this time, one child of his own.

"What about the obligation to study Torah?" asked Reb Yisrael.

"What could I live on?" protested Reb Yozel.

We may imagine that Reb Yisrael pressed Reb Yozel to this effect: "What can you die with?"

We may imagine this because Reb Yisrael reached into Reb Yozel's soul, and disturbed his spiritual equilibrium. Reb Yisrael got Reb Yozel to thinking: I support a family, I study Torah; but still, perhaps I could do more. Perhaps I am not fulfilling my obligation.

Reb Yozel agreed to attend the Musar talks of Reb Yisrael, then about 67, in Memel. Novorodock tradition has it that Reb Yozel heard 13 talks by Reb Yisrael, and then: the third jolt. A self-realization. Reb Yozel could do more—he *must* do more. His life had not been inalterably determined by his prospective father-in-law's death. His talents had not been meant only for the marketplace.

Reb Yisrael urged the young man simply to study more, to trade less. Within every circumstance Reb Yisrael sought balance. It was time to bake *matzos*? Then the interest in *hiddurim* (ritual stringencies) had to be balanced by consideration for the physical hardships that *hiddurim* could impose on bakers. It was necessary to study more? The interest in Torah had to be balanced by the need to support 11 souls.

Something in Reb Yozel rejected this balance. True, he did continue to support his family, but not by studying more and trading less. Reb Yozel had built a substantial trade, and now he turned the capital and the operation over to his wife, devoted himself wholly to Torah and Musar study, and periodically separated from his family.

Why the extreme measures, the imbalance?

Balance requires great strength—strength of mind, strength of will. It is intellectually, even physically demanding always to consider both sides of a question, always to check one's instincts or personal interests in order to respond rationally, from out of full consideration of what Torah demands. It is an effort always to scrutinize one's motives, and to act from out of understanding of what is right, rather than from instinctive jealousy, animosity, or glory-seeking.

Reb Yisrael had that balance.

Reb Yozel knew that he did not.

Reb Yisrael could take two extremes—a meticulous ritual devotion and a refined human sensitivity, for example—and, with precision, act on both.

Reb Yozel knew that he could not.

Reb Yozel knew that he would have to subject his instincts to severe Musar training. He would have to go to one extreme—separation from society—in order to learn to live with joy and freedom within society. He needed "spiritual space" to identify and transcend his unworthy traits and the psychological needs that lay at their base. It would take much difficult work to achieve the spiritual level he sought: freedom *from* impulses not under his control, freedom *to* live in buoyant, jubilant service of Hashem. And so, he separated.

First he separated from business. As one of the first students in the Kovno *Kolel*, he studied for about two years with Reb Itzele Peterburger and Reb Abramchik Tanis. Then he separated from the *Kolel*, periodically repairing to nearby hamlets to study in isolation. In about 1882 came the greatest jolt, and the greatest separation. His wife died in childbirth, whereupon he severed all ties with the Kovno *Kolel*. For one and a half years he neither saw nor spoke to a single person. He sealed himself in a cabin, studied from dawn to dusk into moonlight, prayed, wept, and chastised himself.

What was the ground of his Musar tasks in that cabin? "Jealousy, lust, and glory-seeking" (as *Avos* writes)? Grief? A sense of inadequacy?

There is no way we can know.

The *tzaddik*, purging himself of selfish interests, stripping himself of needs, imbuing himself with purity—with love of *mitzvos* for their own sake—will not readily communicate his specific aspirations and analyses. The Musar disciple's task is not so much to know *what* the *rebbi* seeks as it is to know *that* he seeks, that he works on himself. The disciple's task is to turn the *rebbi*'s example of soul-work into work on his own specific inadequacies.

Reb Yozel's active isolation conveys a general lesson: self-deception and human weakness are formidable opponents, requiring formidable treatment.

Reb Yozel's isolation was scandalous to *maskilim*. With their craving for acceptance by Russian intellectual culture, with their distorted portrayal of Judaism as enlightened rationalism, they had every interest in characterizing Reb Yozel as a traitor to Judaism. If Reb Yozel's intense, spiritual struggles and *perishus* were to be viewed as Jewishly authentic, *maskilim's* efforts to win acceptance for their distortion of Judaism would be damaged.

So defensive were the *maskilim* in their Jewish identity, so treacherous was their desire to remake the Russian image of the Jew, that they denounced Reb Yozel to Tsarist authorities. They wished to make it seem that he was despised by Lithuanian Jewry. To justify their denunciation, they tried to hide counterfeit currency in Reb Yozel's cabin, hoping he would not find it. But he did. When the authorities forcibly entered the cabin to search for currency, they found none. Nonetheless, they forced Reb Yozel to abandon his cabin.

Reb Yozel's most intense period of *perishus* was over.

He had eaten throughout this one-and-a-half-year period thanks to a simple Jew who considered it a privilege to have a part in a *tzaddik's* spiritual growth. If Lithuanian Jewish society included *maskilim* who had lost all sensitivity to absolute spiritual pursuit, it also included ordinary Jews attuned to extraordinary striving and sacrifice.

Reb Yozel knew that he must remarry. Conceivably, he was too emotionally tied to the wife of his youth to want to remarry. But he knew that if he were ever spiritually ready to disseminate his Musar system of radical material renunciation and radical inner joy, he would never succeed if unmarried. Celibacy would be seen as integral to his system; of course it was not.

In consequence Reb Yozel remarried—but to whom?

Consider: By this time, his striving for purity had earned him an outstanding reputation in the Musar circle. A number of brides of means or of lineage (*yichus*) could be his.

Reb Yozel rejected all this. Was the pursuer of spirituality, the disdainer of possessions and of recognition, now to crown himself with wealth and lineage?

Reb Yozel needed someone who understood him, who appreciated his aspirations, who could share in both the renunciation and the joy that he wanted to be their lot. He needed someone who could understand him instinctively, with whom his bond could be unconditional.

One candidate was eminently suitable: the daughter of the simple Jew whose privilege it was to provide his cabin, and to feed him. She knew what her lot would be.

He was willing.

She was willing.

From their partnership, consecrated in about 1883 or 1884, a great movement, and great children, sprang.

I knew one of those children, Rebbetzin Sarah Yaffen, who lived about 100 years, until 1985. The late dean of Yeshivas Chevron, Rabbi Yechezkel Sarna, would look at Rebbetzin Yaffen and say that he saw her father, so strong was their physical resemblance.

Those such as myself who did not know her father looked into her countenance, and her manner, in order to see something else: a spiritual resemblance, a reflection of Novorodock Musar.

Rebbetzin Yaffen was iron-willed, barely able to sit or move, yet able to make the telephone calls necessary to sustain an active *kolel*, able to inspire children, grandchildren, and great-grandchildren to study Torah with devotion, able to compel the publication of contemporary Musar works in both Hebrew and English, able to command the respect—homage, perhaps, is the better word—of *tzaddikim* and yeshiva deans around the world—all because her iron will for Torah and Musar study was, indeed, the reflection of the Novorodock Musar of her father and mother.

When her father and mother married, the dominant aspiration was self-elevation. Reb Yozel spent only Sabbaths at home, and even then spoke only words of Torah. The rest of the week he studied either in isolation or with *ba'alei Musar*. In about 1886, he repaired to the forests in solitude.

Thus life continued for some seven years: isolation, Torah study, introspection, self-criticism, self-improvement, child-raising, silent understanding between husband and wife—climbing the heights of the spirit.

H ow did Reb Yozel live?
As he gradually separated from society, first abandoning his business and eventually studying in isolation—in forests, secret *batei hisbodedus*, and other hidden spots—how did he eat?

Whence his livelihood?

Here we reach the pivot of Novorodock Musar: *bitachon*, "trust in G-d."

Reb Yozel worked so persistently and intensely on *bitachon* that eventually he would sign his name, "B. B., *Ba'al Bitachon*," "master of trust in G-d."

Was this arrogance? Hardly, for under Reb Yozel's conception, there is a concrete criterion according to which success at *bitachon* can be measured.

To Reb Yozel, *bitachon* does not signify the loving acceptance of one's lot, of any and every circumstance brought by Hashem. *Bitachon* is not equanimity in the face of adversity. It is not reading "signs" sent by Hashem. It is not trusting that all will work out for the best, or that Hashem will provide.

To Reb Yozel, *bitachon* was not passive.

It was active.

Bitachon is a means of obtaining what one needs. *Bitachon* is *knowing* that Hashem will provide.

In Reb Yozel's conception, *bitachon* works like this: One sets out to implement a spiritual plan, say, to take one year to improve a single unworthy trait. This requires, say, the intensive study of Torah 12 hours daily, and the study and practice of Musar two hours daily.

Now, how will one live during the year? If one worries about this, one will not turn to the required Torah and Musar. There are two alternatives: to worry about livelihood, and to fail at improving one's unworthy trait; or, to embrace the Musar program, to *expect* that one's livelihood will be provided, and to put every energy into succeeding at improving the unworthy trait.

If one chooses the second alternative, one of two things happens: either one's livelihood materializes, or it does not.

If it does, one's level of *bitachon* is very high indeed.

If it does not, again there are two alternatives: to give up; or, to persist in the Musar program, and to trust that one's livelihood will be provided, while suffering deprivation.

Now the critical point is reached: to know, or to fail to know, that deprivation is *temporary*. If one trusts fully, then Hashem will eventually provide the material conditions that make possible a sustained, genuine effort to reach a spiritual goal.

Trust, then, can be measured: either one's livelihood for the duration of a spiritual program is provided, or it is not.

One knows whether one is a master of *bitachon*, or whether one is not.

In response to incredulous reactions to his description of *bitachon*, Reb Yozel in his old age simply said: "Look at me. Am I alive? Am I healthy? I lived for years in *perishus*, in forests, and I did not starve."

In other words: If one persists at *bitachon*, it works. *Bitachon* provides.

Its success depends on how deep is one's yearning, how pervasive one's aspiration. It depends on whether the immediate deprivation, or the prospect of spiritual elevation, dominates one's consciousness.

Once the spiritual goal overwhelms the consciousness, the immediate deprivations lose their sting; and sooner or later the fruits of *bitachon* become palpable. From here or there, the livelihood comes. This or that becomes the emissary of Hashem to supply the spiritual seeker, the *ba'al bitachon*, with the minimal resources to enable him to persist in his quest.

When Reb Yozel decided to enter his cabin, first he *decided*; only afterwards did the simple Jew step forward to offer to feed him.

First comes the decision, the determination, the absolute commitment to seek a spiritual goal in Torah and Musar, and only then comes the necessary support.

When the decision to pursue a spiritual goal is adhered to, *bitachon* yields fruits.

When the decision is not adhered to, *bitachon* appears to be a phantom.

Once I was standing with Rabbi Eliezer Ben Zion Bruk at a bus stop on Shmuel Hanavi St., in Jerusalem, in front of his yeshiva. We were waiting and waiting. Though he never complained about his limp—he was wounded during the Israeli War of Independence—it bothered him.

And here we were, waiting and waiting.

Suddenly Rabbi Bruk turned and said:

"Reb Hillel, if I were a real *ba'al bitachon*, someone in a car would come along right now to offer me a ride."

Bitachon: a spiritual endeavor with concrete, measurable results.

Bitachon: an active trusting in Hashem to provide the means to achieve worthy spiritual goals. *Bitachon*: a process which can entail deprivation, but which sooner or later frees the genuine seeker after Hashem from all worry.

Initially a technique for obtaining material support, *bitachon* eventually soothes the spiritual seeker, instilling a serenity that pervades his demeanor. In its fullest sense, Reb Yozel's signature, "B. B., Ba'al Bitachon," signified his freedom from disturbance by any material condition or external circumstance.

Bitachon: the liberating technique at the basis of all that Reb Yozel became and achieved.

Bitachon liberates from material need.

What about psychological needs?

Here is where the special strength of mind, courage of analysis, and agility of soul—that special discipline we call Musar—enters. In Reb Yozel's conception, *bitachon* brings material support alone. There is no *bitachon* in the realm of the spirit. There is no trusting in Hashem to supply spiritual elevation. That comes only from repair of character and pursuit of piety.

Bitachon supplies the minimal material conditions for soul work, but the work itself is the goal of Musar, the task of the *ba'al Musar*.

Reb Yozel's audacious, utter reliance on Hashem was his *bitachon*. His supreme effort was his discipline and self-scrutiny, his relentless work on himself.

Reb Yozel's techniques of Musar were many: to study Musar books; to analyze oneself by oneself, yet also in the presence of a friend, and of a groups of friends; to trade ideas with friends in analysis of character generally, and of one's own character particularly; to share all of one's possessions, even to give them away, so as not to be dependent on them; to embarrass oneself intentionally, so as to learn to withstand embarrassment.

"Not to be embarrassed before the mockers" is the first law in the Code of Jewish Law (*Shulchan Aruch*) and the first law—as well as the pinnacle—of Novorodock Musar. When one can perform *mitzvos* without regard to the status or suffering they bring, utterly oblivious to the praise or blame they elicit, one is a free man—or woman—before Hashem.

This, then, is Reb Yozel's goal: total freedom. Freedom from material want through *bitachon*, freedom from psychological want through embarrassment before Hashem alone.

On this level of serenity, a person can withstand everything: slave labor in Siberia, Nazi deprivation, separation from family, food shortages, absence of sewage facilities, extended chaos—literally everything, except the barrel of a loaded gun pointed at the head.

And sometimes even that.

The year was 1918 or 1919. Reb Yozel's telegram read, simply, "Merciful Father." A few of his disciples managed to pirate the message safely past Red Army lines to isolated disciples. They had requested guidance in light of Bolshevik soldiers' threat to murder them for studying Torah and Musar. To the isolated Novorodockers, the message was clear.

A few days later, Bolshevik soldiers burst into the Novorodock yeshiva. The commanding officer marched straight to the head Novorodocker, pulled his gun, and demanded the yeshiva's immediate closure. The young Musarnik rose from his seat, unbuttoned his shirt, held it open, and, fully composed, said: "Shoot." The younger students lined up behind him, unbuttoned their shirts, and squared off in silence. They were placid and defiant.

The soldiers, accustomed to seeing anguish before their deadly gunfire, were apparently thrown off balance. Perhaps they were awestruck. Perhaps they harbored a certain respect for the fearless students. In any case, they turned and left.

Novorodockers had once again survived confrontation with death.

Reb Yozel had turned his radical Musar analysis into a program for ordinary Jews in extraordinary times. From the forests of Slobodka he had built a personal will so strong that he took his message to the masses.

From the concentrated attention he had paid to his own unworthy traits, in his isolated life of solitude, he built the energy whose explosion brought a new power to thousands of Jewish youngsters subjected to Marxist materialism.

When he left the forests in about 1893 or 1894, he reached the level necessary for disseminating Torah and Musar. He then proved, retroactively, that his reclusive study and self-scrutiny had been a preparation "to turn the many to righteousness."

He returned to the world as a new man.

He returned to society with an inner release, a clarity of purpose, a zest for life—with an utter freedom from the temptations and empty pursuits of society. He set in motion the most sustained growth of the Musar movement since Reb Yisrael Salanter had come to Kovno four decades earlier.

What others saw as impossible, or dared not even dream possible, Reb Yozel now accomplished. Throwing himself into public activity as zealously as he had once thrown himself into isolated study, he founded nine yeshivas in two years, 1894 to 1895, all under the nominal supervision of Reb Itzele Peterburger.

Then, in 1896, he struck out on his own. He opened his first yeshiva in a suburb of Minsk, Lithuania, in "Novogrudock," *Novorodock* in the Musar vernacular.

From 1896 to 1914, as the Novorodock yeshiva grew, Reb Yozel molded seven major disciples, two of whom became his sons-in-law, Rabbis Avraham Yaffen and Yisrael Yaakov Lubchansky. With the outbreak of World War I, Reb Yozel and his major disciples began a revolution of their own.

Reb Yozel turned evil to opportunity.

It was clear that Germany would conquer Novorodock. The city's material fate would rise and its spiritual fate would sink, said Reb Yozel. It was better to place the yeshiva at the mercies of starvation in Russia than of *Haskalah* under Germany.

Without means or help, Reb Yozel and his students made their way eastward into Russia, to Gomel. Under the press of widespread food shortages and general chaos, other yeshivas closed, and their students passed through Gomel, a crossroads. The transplanted Novorodock yeshiva took all comers, and grew to hundreds. When the contending armies came to draft Novorodock's students, Reb Yozel scattered them to the hinterlands—a blessing in disguise. The Novorodockers proceeded to found a new yeshiva wherever they went. Novorodock grew without stop.

When "progromists" of all stripes struck at Jews, Novorodockers simply uprooted themselves and founded yeshivas elsewhere. Daunted by nothing, with everything around them collapsing, they gathered some 2000 students. At the end of the war, when Reb Yozel had to transfer the central Novorodock yeshiva from Gomel to Kiev, his disciples promptly established five branches throughout Kiev, notwithstanding widespread starvation, a flood of refugees, and a plague.

Against every odd, Reb Yozel expanded both the numbers and the borders of the Musar movement.

He met head on the increasingly dominant challenge of Marxist materialism. The material world is everything? "What you see is what you get"? The tangible is exhaustive?

For this philosophical foundation of Marxism, Reb Yozel had not merely disdain. He had an answer: *the worl ! is nothing; what you see is but an intimation of the sacred Reality you get; the tangible is a speck in an infinite Mercy*. And he had an answer not merely in theory.

He had one in practice.

He could live without material possessions—so could scores of disciples.

He could live in profound serenity with spiritual pursuit alone—so could scores of disciples.

He could trust in Hashem with such determination that, in hardship bordering on starvation, he could expand the circle of his influence; he could increase the numbers of his yeshivas; he could take minds off tattered clothing and black-bread diets.

He could say: *Yesharim darchei Hashem*, "the ways of Hashem are upright; the righteous stride forth in them, the unrighteous stumble in them. " He could say: In every circumstance, take strides in the ways of Hashem, for from uprightness, only good can come forth. He could say, "Merciful Father, *Av HaRachamim*"—he could tell his disciples to commit themselves to the martyrdom commemorated in the Sabbath prayer of *Av HaRachamim*. He could say this because he knew that in following the ways of Hashem, only good could come forth.

Not only did he know it.

His disciples knew it.

Still more: He knew that his disciples knew.

He knew that Novorodock Musar worked. He knew that once a youngster was swept up in the inspiriting Novorodock atmosphere of intellectual mastery of Talmud and single-minded search for self-knowledge and joy, that youngster was transformed.

He knew that he had built a network of such tight mutual understanding that a mere two-word message could contain all he needed to communicate to disciples in extremity.

Reb Yozel knew that he had discovered the proper path not only for himself, but for a significant segment of his generation.

Fire.
Reb Yozel spread Novorodock Musar through Russia with burning zeal—with urgency, sacrifice, and concentrated energy. He put his fiery spirit into pungent aphorisms.

Urgency:

"When it is necessary to send a letter, I send a telegram; when it is necessary to send a telegram, I send an emissary; when it is necessary to send an emissary, I go myself. "

"I never ask myself whether I *can* do something, only whether I *need* to do something."

Sacrifice:

"I am astonished that a person can ever bring himself to say: 'This is mine.' "

"One who gives actually receives more than a recipient. A recipient acquires something material and limited; one who gives acquires a pure heart."

Concentrated energy:

"If a person devoted himself to the public welfare as much as he does to his family, he could found 100 yeshivas."

Reb Yozel snatched from Marxist persecution the disciples who went on to found nearly 100 yeshivas in the 1920s and 1930s.

For what?

For *love of life:*

"A person must relinquish all of his tomorrows for one today, lest he come to relinquish all of his todays for one tomorrow."

"Even the worst of the present is more beautiful than the best of the future."

Reb Yozel put his fiery spirit into compelling aphorisms because his mind turned every analysis of the self, and every inquiry into Torah, to action. Deed. Practicality. *Jews are starving out there*, Reb Yozel said, *starved by a destructive educational system*. He said that it is time to act, to turn every talent, every twist of mind and twinge of conscience, to *zikkui harabbim*, "turning the many to righteousness."

Any Jew has the potential to do the job.

"In war time, even a simple soldier can become a general."

In the war for Torah Judaism one becomes a general by being decisive.

"There are three types of dishes: milk, meat, and *pareve*. But there are only two types of people: those who proceed on the right path, and those who do not. In people, there is no *pareve*."

How does one get to the right path?

"All my life I have taught man to be a seeker."

But is it not frightening always to be dissatisfied in matters of the spirit—always to be seeking a higher level?

"This world is a very narrow span. Cross it—if you're unafraid, you can."

Fear stifles action.

Fearlessness prompts it. The seeker after the right path becomes fearless, in worldly as well as spiritual matters. When Reb Yozel dispensed with sending an emissary and "went himself," he often rode underneath or on top of speeding railroad cars commandeered by contending Bolshevik and counter-revolutionary armies. No matter. Urgency required the trip; sacrifice was its necessity; concentrated energy, its means. "This world is a very narrow span; cross it—if you're unafraid, you can."

Madregas HaAdam, *The Stature of Man*, is Reb Yozel's masterpeice. He put his spirit to pungent aphorisms, but also to much more. He produced one of the most significant works ever to spring from the Musar movement.

Delivered as a series of 12 lectures in 1919 shortly before he died, transcribed and then printed in 12 separate pamphlets for the next 28 years, and finally published in one volume in 1947, *Madregas HaAdam* shines as a monument to intellectual coherence and comprehensiveness.

The book is airtight in its logic and unrestrained in its passion. It shows how Reb Yozel fired so many souls to face down fear, to take every risk to disseminate Torah and Musar. *Madregas HaAdam* demonstrates that Reb Yozel did not merely manufacture sermons. He probed the words of the Sages (*Chazal*) for everything instructive to the state of his soul and the state of Jewish society. He set before himself several major tasks, the achievement of any one of which would justify his stature as a major Musar thinker. He built a philosophy of Jewish ethical history; a psychology of personal transformation; a theology and technique of *bitachon*; and a philosophy and technique of outreach to Jews threatened by assimilation, or already assimilated.

Madregas HaAdam draws on *Chazal*, on Musar thinkers of the ages, and on Reb Yisrael Salanter. The originality and achievement of *Madregas HaAdam* are its totality of vision and richness of technique. Reb Yozel writes not only what a Jew should do, but also how he can do it.

For example, in the twelfth and concluding chapter of *Madregas HaAdam*,[1] Reb Yozel asks and answers ten questions about how to stimulate all Torah Jews to reach out to all other Jews. The ten questions:

1. Is there an educational regimen to train qualified educators for outreach?
2. Must such an educator take upon himself even the material burdens needed to succeed?
3. Can a person exempt himself from outreach, saying that it rests only on the *gedolei hador*, the great Torah scholars in the generation?
4. Is there a justification for *anyone* exempting himself from outreach?
5. Does the Torah require an educator to uproot himself continually to disseminate Torah?
6. Can individuals influence the whole world simply by the strength of spiritual conviction?
7. Must an educator take an interest in everything that pertains to youth, and scrutinize their every action, with a view to correction?
8. Does work in outreach counter personal growth in Torah?
9. Must an educator thoroughly know the Jews to be reached before acting?
10. Can a person exempt himself from outreach on the grounds that the responsibility is too great?

When I studied *Madregas HaAdam* with Rabbi Bruk, and later

---

1. This has been felicitously translated by Shraga Silverstein as *To Turn the Many to Righteousness* (Feldheim, 1972).

with Rabbi Orlansky, I felt the power of Reb Yozel. For decades he put his mind to figuring out how to turn the likes and dislikes of teenagers and young adults to greatness in Torah and Musar. From the fire of his spirit and the psychological perceptivity of his mind he produced giants: the Steipler *Rav*, whose legendary dedication to Torah study reflected the aspiration to greatness of Novorodock Musar; Rabbi Abraham Yaffen, whose Talmudic scholarship received the power to nurture a system of nearly 100 yeshivas from Novorodock Musar; Rabbi Yisrael Yaakov Lubchansky, a *mashgiach* whose *temimus* or wholeheartedness left an indelible imprint on countless disciples of Novorodock Musar; Rabbi Yitzchak Orlansky, the *mashgiach* in the Novorodock branch in Minsk in which the Steipler *Rav* was yeshiva dean. What a yeshiva that must have been!

When I studied *Madregas HaAdam*, I established contact with a visionary.

"According to the pain is the gain" (*lefum tza'ara agra*). Novorodock Musar's achievements resulted from great—almost unimaginably great—effort. In Novorodock yeshivas, Musar study was not just reading words; the training of disciples was not just teaching them Torah; the founding of scores of yeshivas was not just traveling from place to place and gathering students.

Musar study

Its point in Novorodock was to dig into the soul. Quiet contemplation had its role, but it was minor. To escape the countless temptations that sprung from almost every circumstance and inner impulse, the honest Musar student had to feel anguish. He had to know how thoroughly the unworthy temptations permeated him, how utterly they suffused him. He had to face the reality of the soil on his soul. He had to see it to want to overcome it. He had to feel its iron grip to want to break it.

Musar study was the opportunity for blunt self-confrontation, for honest—and therefore painful—analysis. Musar study was to set before the eyes the gap between the lofty purity that Musar study could deliver, and the lowly impurity that continually made itself felt in lust for pleasure, desire for material goods, yearning for recognition, and urges to be arrogant, selfish, or manipulative. The task was immense, the goal was reachable.

Musar study, undertaken honestly and abundantly, could remake anybody.

And so, in Novorodock yeshivas, Musar study was a time of intense self-examination. It entailed crying, shouting, humming, singing—anything to get the emotions up to the surface, to get one's true feelings—one's real personal qualities—up before the eyes and the mind, the tool of self-analysis.

Musar study entailed putting the soul on the table, to be judged. "Non-judgmental" was a word unknown to Novorodockers. The question was not whether to judge, but how to judge well, evaluate properly, and analyze sensitively.

Musar study had to be done both publicly and privately, in the *beis ha-Musar* and the *beis hisbodedus*. It required the collective attention of Musar comrades and the lonely solitude of a searching soul. Even after Reb Yozel left his concentrated solitude, he maintained a *beis hisbodedus* in every city in which he lived. Novorodockers received a message: Every true Musar student should reserve time for solitude.

The task being immense, the road to success was long.

Long—but finite.

Musar study could work. The seeker could grow. Unworthy qualities could be improved. Great people could emerge.

They could—and they did.

Training disciples

Its point in Novorodock was to shape a teacher of Torah and Musar, to train someone who could transmit to others all that he had learned. Reb Yozel's students were not "students"; they were potential leaders.

The entire Novorodock program conspired to make every student aspire to be a leader. The curriculum of the yeshiva included programs that stressed mutual responsibility.

Example: forensic training. Every Novorodock student received instruction in public speaking. Reb Yozel was a spellbinding orator. He knew its importance in disseminating Torah. He made it an integral part of the Novorodock curriculum.

I never met a Novorodocker who could not hold an audience: Rabbi Hillel Vitkind with his fire and soul-penetrating passion; Rabbi Orlansky with his warmth and wonder; Rabbi Bruk with his simple, utter clarity and simple, hammering phrases; Rabbi Nekritz with his balance and thoughtfulness.

Example: teaching. Every Novorodock student received pedagogic training. They taught either younger students who had just arrived in the yeshiva, or students in the faraway towns to which Novorodockers were dispatched. Reb Yozel knew the importance of first-rate pedagogy in disseminating Torah. He made its acquisition an integral part of the Novorodock curriculum.

With everyone in Novorodock striving not only to perfect himself but to introduce others to Musar discipline, Reb Yozel created an atmosphere in which he produced great leaders, major disciples: Rabbis Avraham Yaffen, Yoel Baranchik, David Bliacher, David Budnick, Shmuel Weintrob, Avraham Zalmans, and Yisrael Yaakov Lubchansky.

Rabbi Yaffen was Reb Yozel's right-hand man in the central Novorodock yeshiva. Each of the others (except Rabbi Lubchansky) founded a yeshiva network first centered around a Russian city, and then, after the Novorodock flight to Poland in 1922, a Polish or Latvian city. Rabbi Lubchansky became the communal rabbi of Baranowitz, in whose great yeshiva, headed by Rabbi Elchanan Wasserman, he also served as *mashgiach*.

From these bearers of Reb Yozel's spirit came the Novorodock explosion.

Founding yeshivas

Its point in Novorodock was to reach students—nothing else. Not to build an image. Not to construct a building. To Novorodockers, a "yeshiva" was only sometimes a building. Novorodockers came to a city, entered a synagogue, gathered students. Torah and Musar study began at once, usually in a local synagogue. Often there was no room for the entire student body in one location. Often students slept on synagogue benches, and had no regular meals.

No matter. Students studied Torah. This was of the essence; all the rest was secondary.

The thirst for spiritual elevation was immense. Poverty notwithstanding, Novorodock flourished. In fact, it grew so large that Reb Yozel had to institute a formal structure to unify the movement.

Novorodock hosted conventions with representatives from each Novorodock branch. These conventions, first held in the midst of World War I, laid the foundation for the outreach that proceeded with unrestrained enthusiasm after the war. These conventions unified the Novorodock curriculum (*Madregas HaAdam* was the culmination of this effort), and created elite units to lead the way in both studying and disseminating the Novorodock *derech* or orientation.

The fortitude of this elite leadership was sorely tested.

First, Reb Yozel died in 1919. A plague had stricken Kiev, and Reb Yozel rejected all pleas to remove himself from Novorodock's improvised nursing teams. He could not ask anyone to do anything he himself would not do. He treated his students, contracted typhus, and died.

Second, the Bolsheviks tightened the noose, imprisoning Novorodockers, including even Reb Yozel's successor, Rabbi Avraham Yaffen.

But nothing stopped Novorodock. When there was no leader, Reb Yozel's disciples took over. When there was no place—not even a broken down synagogue—Novorodockers studied in cemeteries! When Bolshevik persecution turned to violence, they consulted the Chafetz Chaim, then undertook a daring, dangerous flight to Poland—the flight whose details Rabbi Bruk revealed to me. It was in Poland, from 1922 to 1939, that Reb Yozel's major disciples spread throughout the countryside from centers in Bialystock, Mezritsch, Warsaw, Minsk, and Latvia to found 89 yeshivas.

When an unspeakably evil Austrian creature, may his name and memory be blotted out, came and did what he did, some Novorodockers, such as Rabbis Yehudah Leib Nekritz and Yitzchak Orlansky, escaped from Poland to Siberia, while some others survived in killing camps. These Novorodockers squeezed from their reservoir of spiritual stubbornness every last energy to live according to Torah, to bake *matzos*, to pray daily, to observe the Sabbath, even to build *sukkos*. And when the horror finished its course, Novorodockers persisted in theirs. Perhaps the most astounding tale I ever heard about these indomitable disciples of Reb Yozel . . . perhaps I should not have been surprised, since, after all, these were people who, in "normal extremity," studied in cemeteries . . . After World War II, Novorodockers who survived Siberia made their way back across Europe. Throughout the trek, they studied Torah. When one group happened upon German soil, there was no place to study— simply no available building.

With a single exception.

An empty concentration camp, not yet sanitized, was available. The scent of the flesh, so to speak, was still there.

The inheritors of the fortitude and the faith of Reb Yozel—the disciple of Reb Yisrael Salanter who could scrape out of his soul every last perversity the world could implant in it, who could thus discover laughter and love—these inheritors entered that concentration camp. They sat down, opened the sacred books, and did the deed that signals the eternal victory of Jews and Judaism over every opponent.

They sat in *simchah*, in that profane place, to study the holy Torah. They performed a *mitzvah*, notwithstanding the unspeakable, emotional obstacle. *Kiyyum haTorah*, observance of the Torah: this was the Novorodockers' goal, the climax of their struggle. *Simchah*: this was the Novorodocker's inner state, the reward for their struggle.

9.

Slobodka Musar

The sheer grace, delicacy, and purity of Rabbi Yaakov Moshe Lesin can never leave me.

His piety, hidden and humble as it was, restrained and reticent as it was, struck me from the first moment I saw him. Rabbi Lesin was the first Musar personality I ever encountered. I noticed him the first or second day I arrived in New York City in 1965 to study at Yeshiva University.

Here I was in upper Manhattan, a bustling, crowded, and dirty place, with uneven sidewalks, refuse strewn about, and graffiti sprayed in no order or style all over the buildings along the streets.

All this—and Rabbi Lesin.

This saintly man appeared almost as if an apparition, a dream, an embodiment of gentleness and richness of soul that persisted beyond the destruction of East European Jewry. I had always tried to imagine that world. Now I could see one of its exemplary representatives.

I watched Rabbi Lesin, his every step, gesture, and nod. They were perfectly measured, perfectly calculated, yet also graceful. Only much later did I learn that in Slobodka Musar it was a high ideal to control each thought and act, to consider the consequences of each motion of mind or body, before committing it to reality. Right then, when I first encountered Slobodka Musar in the demeanor of Rabbi Lesin, I learned that calculation and carefulness did not exclude gentleness and grace.

Rabbi Lesin generated an aura of imperturbable serenity. It was no more possible to imagine him unsettled than it was to imagine him eating unkosher food. His noble service of Hashem seemed to get lost in the bustle of students always hurrying here and there, trying to keep apace of the heavy demands made upon them. The world does not pay much attention to refinement. Rabbi Lesin was from another world, another time; he spoke another language, occupied himself with lofty matters—with piety, with Musar, with devotion in prayer, purity of heart.

Everything about Rabbi Lesin bespoke *romemus*, exaltedness. When he prayed, he appeared to pull together every thought and deed of the past minutes or hours, offering up this segment of his life as if it were a sacrifice (which he, as a *kohen* or priest, would have offered in the holy Temple centuries ago). When he recited a blessing over the Torah, it seemed as if his voice, a creation of sheer musical purity, called into the presence of all who heard it the chosenness (*asher bachar banu*) and the eternity (*chayyei olam nata besocheinu*) of each Jew. When he gave his evening Musar *shmues* at 9:40 pm, it seemed as if his yearning for ethical perfection reached up from wellsprings so deep that nothing but yearning for holiness existed in him.

Only much later did I learn that in Slobodka it was a deliberate pedagogical technique to teach by indirection, to touch the soul of the disciple by not confronting it, by penetrating around and behind the defenses that the disciple erected. Other teachers at Yeshiva University had a more direct and measurable impact than Rabbi Lesin, but as I encounter students of Torah and Jews in the professions in cities large and small, in Israel and America, I am amazed how many share their feelings about this quiet son of Slobodka; how his hushed, graceful yearning and *hisromemus* penetrated to the quick, touched the deepest, the most enduring level of being.

This was Slobodka Musar: a way of fashioning an exalted spirit with the lightest of touch—the lightest, and on that score the most penetrating.

Slobodka Musar penetrated.

It motivated.

It produced piety and brilliance, beyond belief. How could one yeshiva—a small wooden building in a small and indistinguished suburb of Kovno, Lithuania—produce such giants as Rabbis Aharon Kotler, Reuven Grozovsky Yaakov Kaminecki, Yitzhak Hutner, and Yitzhak Yaakov Ruderman?

To name the graduates of Slobodka most familiar to American Jews is to name only a few of its distinguished graduates. There were others of the highest stature who made their mark in Europe and Israel—Rabbis Alter Shmuelevitz, Eliezer Yehudah Finkel, Yechezkel Sarna, Yechiel Yaakov Weinberg, Yitzhak Aizik Sher—and in America in an earlier time—Rabbis Shlomo Heiman, David Leibowitz.

This is a "who's who" in early- and mid-twentieth century leadership in the Ashkenazi yeshiva world—the deans of Kletsk, Lakewood, Chaim Berlin, Ner Israel, Mir, Chevron, Slobodka, Berlin. Even so, these are only a few of the first-rank yeshiva deans, communal rabbis, rabbinical judges, and *mashgichim* who graduated from Slobodka. By the onset of World War II, the alumni association of Slobodka numbered hundreds of first-rank *talmidei chachamim* who held positions of major responsibility in Europe (West and East), America, and Palestine.

What was the secret of Slobodka?

It was utterly simple and utterly complex.

Utterly simple: one man.

Utterly complex: what a man! The Alter of Slobodka, Rabbi Nosson Zvi Finkel. Orphan. Pedagogic genius. Master of Torah lore. Visionary of Talmudic scholarship. Leader *par excellence*. Also: ascetic, introspective, hidden.

A mystery.

What was Slobodka's secret? This is not the question. *Who was the Alter of Slobodka?*

This is the question.

To one Moshe Finkel, whom we know to have been Nosson Zvi Finkel's father, Nosson Zvi Finkel was born, in 1849, in the city of Rassein, whose rabbi we know to have been Alexander Moshe Lapidus, disciple of Reb Yisrael Salanter.

City, date, name of father, name of rabbi: these and these alone we know of the Alter of Slobodka's childhood. At a young age his parents died; an uncle in Vilna raised him; at 15 he was a young Talmud scholar, attractive to prospective fathers-in-law: this is known. His teachers, schools, friends, relatives—his books, interests, mannerisms, ideas—all this is unknown.

The Alter's beginnings, like his life, are a mystery.

From Rassein, via Vilna, Reb Nota Hirsh (as the Alter was then called) went to Kelm since a distinguished Jew there, Meir Bashis, took this talented teenager for his son-in-law, who then studied Torah in Kelm for several years. From Kelm, via other stopping points, Reb Nota Hirsh went back to Rassein since he, even as a teenager, was an effective orator, in demand in outlying towns. From Rassein, where, as an orator, he attracted the attention of Rabbi Alexander Moshe Lapidus, he came back to Kelm, since Rabbi Lapidus asked him to deliver a letter to Rabbi Simcha Zisl Ziv, in Kelm.

The letter, unbeknownst to its bearer, introduced Reb Nota Hirsh to Rabbi Simcha Zisl as a potential jewel of Musar.

Rabbi Simcha Zisl immediately took Reb Nota Hirsh aside to enter into deep discussion—a discussion that affected Reb Nota

Hirsh so profoundly that he spent the night in tears, deciding then and there to devote his life to study of Torah and fear of Heaven.

Rabbi Simcha Zisl devoted special attention to Reb Nota Hirsh, whose capacity to absorb the Musar approach was phenomenal, whose ability to apply that approach as a Musar leader himself was even more phenomenal. He played major roles in the Musar movement almost simultaneously with his arrival in Kelm, innocently bearing a letter from one disciple of Reb Yisrael Salanter to another. It is as if from the moment Reb Nota Hirsh Finkel entered the Musar circle, he became "the Alter of Slobodka."

With oratorical prowess from his youth and Musar from Rabbi Simcha Zisl, the Alter turned to the students of Reb Leizer Gordon in Kelm and encouraged them in Torah study and the Musar discipline. When word of his effectiveness reached Rabbi Simcha Zisl, Rabbi Simcha Zisl appointed him to an administrative post in the Beis Hatalmud of Kelm.

The "Alter" was then only in his early twenties.

His pedagogical prowess was so pronounced that when Rabbi Simcha Zisl moved Beis Hatalmud from Kelm to Grubin in 1876, his protege went with him.

He remained only a short time. As Reb Yozel, the Alter of Novorodock, respected Rabbi Simcha Zisl highly, but went his own way, so too did the Alter of Slobodka. At 28, he began to found his own institutions.

He opened a precursor of a *kolel* in Slobodka in 1877. Each evening, Musar study and mutual personal analysis capped the day's studies. In 1878 he founded another institution for single students. When the Kovno *Kolel* of Rabbis Yisrael Salanter and Yitzchak Elchanan Spektor opened in 1879, the Alter joined the administration, contributing to the *Kolel*'s financial and educational advancement.

Active in two *kolelim* and a yeshiva, he also became the *mashgiach* or spiritual supervisor in Or Hachaim, a yeshiva for youngsters in Slobodka. There, he instituted a formal curriculum, steadied finances, and weeded out unfit students. In 1881 he brokered the financing for the foundation of the Telshe yeshiva, which Reb Leizer Gordon developed two years later. Finally, in 1882, when he was 32, he founded the yeshiva of Slobodka.

What a background he brought to the job!

He had experience teaching youngsters from his position as *mashgiach* in Or Hachaim (which he turned into a feeder yeshiva to Slobodka); he had experience teaching both older youth and married scholars; he had experience in administration and fundraising; he was adept at public speaking. Most of all, he had an image of what the new yeshiva student should be, and a solid idea of why it should be that way. The Alter was not "merely" an organizational master; he was a visionary.

Our best access to his vision is the single article he published in his lifetime, the introduction to *Etz Peri* (1881), a volume issued to garner support for the fledgling Kovno *Kolel*. Parenthetically, this volume contains Reb Yisrael Salanter's clearest formulation of his psychology of the unconscious. Our interest now is the Alter's introduction.

The Alter saw a crisis. More accurately, he was personally devastated by his sense of that crisis. *Haskalah*, as he put it poignantly, "chilled" and "froze" commitment to Torah. It generated, minimally, a stilling of the "sacred emotion" of Judaism. Maximally, it generated denial of G-d or repudiation of *mitzvos*, or both.

The point was not an individual argument of *Haskalah* here or there; the point was *Haskalah*'s effect.

The point, in short, was the future of *klal yisrael*. Without serious dedication to Torah study, *klal yisrael* was doomed. *Haskalah* was robbing young people of the will to that dedication.

Today we see, sadly, intermarriage and ignorance. The Alter saw the steps that could lead to this. We have become accustomed to a state of defection from *klal yisrael*; the Alter saw it happening. He personally took it upon himself to put his talents—his life—to reversing the erosion of commitment to Torah.

The alternatives, said the Alter, were simple.

Either one sat in satisfaction, worried only about oneself, not about one's generation; or, one assumed the responsibility to magnify the name of the Holy One, Blessed be He, "throughout the world, from one end to the other. "

Like the Alter of Novorodock, the Alter of Slobodka worked in conditions of extreme poverty, but unlike the Alter of Novorodock, the Alter of Slobodka chose not to turn poverty to an opportunity to work on *bitachon*.

He wished to dignify the image of the yeshiva student.

To give his students a steady diet, to get them into decent, unpatched clothing, to get them off the bench in the local synagogue and into a real bed—all this was not only an aspiration to help his students. It was a program to make Torah study respectable, so that Jewish youth could be won back to it.

The Alter weeded out weaker students not because he believed that Torah study was not for everyone. With *klal yisrael* in crisis, the Alter had to guarantee first-rank Torah scholarship for coming generations. The elite would have to be the object of his energy.

He knew how to mobilize financial and Musar resources. He gained the ear of patrons of Musar, of Reb Shraga Feivel Frank and Eliezer Yaakov Chavas. He studied under Rabbi Simcha Zisl, he brought students to Reb Itzele Peterburger, he had Rabbi Naftali Amsterdam join his first *kolel*, he associated closely with Reb Abramchik Tanis and helped the yeshiva of Reb Leizer Gordon. At one time or another he studied under all of these Musar luminaries or brought students to them. Musar was in the air, with hidden attics and out-of-the-way, small synagogues supplementing the formal Musar institutions, all of which were mobilized—or founded by—the Alter of Slobodka.

If the state of Torah is finally gaining good ground, the success can be traced as much to the Alter of Slobodka—his vision and pedagogic genius—as to any other person.

For his vision bore fruit.

Hashem took Hebrew slaves out of Egypt with a "strong hand." Maimonides subtitled his masterful, 14-book *Mishneh Torah* or Code of Jewish Law *The Strong Hand, Hayad Hachazakah*, since the Hebrew letters whose numerical value add up to 14 are *yad*, "hand."

Attribute of Hashem and codification of His law, *yad chazakah* acquired a third connotation in 1897. It entered the annals of Talmudic scholarship as one of the most remarkable young groups ever to study Hashem's law.

There were 14 scholars in the group, the Alter of Slobodka's *yad chazakah*, which did not even exhaust Slobodka's intellectual elite.

By 1897, Slobodka had acquired a depth and breadth to enable it to apportion its human treasures among new or struggling yeshivas all over Lithuania, even into Russia. In 1897, Rabbi Yaakov David Willowski ("Ridbaz"), rabbi of Slutsk, asked the Alter to help him establish a yeshiva. The Alter responded by dispatching one of his two *rashei yeshiva*, Rabbi Isser Zalman Meltzer—and his *yad chazakah*, his 14, budding Talmudic giants. Among them:

• Eliezer Yehudah Finkel (the Alter's son), later yeshiva dean in Mir.

• Alter Shmuelevitz, later Talmudic lecturer in Novorodock and Shetzutzin (father of the late yeshiva dean and Musar master in Jerusalem, Rabbi Chaim Shmuelevitz).

• Yosef Eliyahu Henkin, later *posek* and head of Ezras Torah in New York.

• Reuven Katz, later chief rabbi of Petach Tikvah.

• Rabbi Pesach Pruskin, later rabbi and yeshiva dean in Shklov, rabbi in Amtsislav and Kobrin—and *rebbi* of the late, towering Rabbi Moshe Feinstein.

Slobodka became a national resource, taking the place of Volozhin (closed in 1892 by Tsarist decree), actively nurturing or founding major yeshivas. Among them:

• Slutsk, under Rabbi Isser Zalman Meltzer.

• Kletsk, under Rabbi Aharon Kotler.

• Mir, under Rabbis Eliezer Yehudah Finkel and Yerucham Levovitz.

• Maltsh, under Rabbi Shimon Shkop.

• Shetzutzin, under Rabbis Leib Chasman and Alter Shmuelevitz.

• Grodno, under the Alter's son, Shmuel Finkel.

- Lodz, under Rabbi Shlomo Grodzinski and others—the first seed of the Musar movement in Poland.
- Shklov, under Rabbi Avraham Noach Palei—the first seed of the Musar movement in Russia.

Slobodka fostered the interdependence of yeshivas. In Slobodka's early years, the Alter sent his better students to Rabbi Simcha Zisl Ziv's Beis Hatalmud for ripening and maturation. Later, when Slobodka founded or aided other yeshivas, they sent students to Slobodka for ripening and maturation.

The Alter's point was not his yeshiva, it was his students. It was to train effective and extensive Torah leadership, to create a variety of resources—of yeshivas and *talmidei chachamim*—each to be tapped for help by whomever needed it, each to be helped by whomever could extend it. Under the Alter, Slobodka became more than a yeshiva. It became a nerve center for Torah scholarship throughout Lithuania, even beyond.

With Slobodka, the Alter created a first. He turned Slobodka into the first major *yeshiva gedolah* or post-high school yeshiva in the Musar movement. He established the first major medium for Musar that reached actively and extensively into the community, and that demonstrated the unity of Torah study and Musar study not just for *yechidei segulah* or special individuals. Reb Yisrael Salanter's quest for an effective medium to sustain Musar found its culmination in the Musar yeshiva, first sustained by the Alter of Slobodka.

Two phenomena fashioned Slobodka's cutting edge: the Alter's dedication and insight, and Rabbi Moshe Mordechai Epstein's intellect and clarity.

In the search to identify the secret of the Alter's pedagogic genius, it is possible to overlook the obvious: the Alter's dedication.

For thirty years, 1876 to 1906, the Alter virtually never left Slobodka. He not only studied with students, he lived with them. He visited his family—in Kelm—only twice yearly (*Pesach* and *Sukkos*). Even after 1906, when his family lived in the yeshiva, it occupied only two small rooms. The Alter gave every energy to his students.

He observed and counseled them; he devised ways endlessly to tap their strongest qualities.

He observed them not simply in the classroom, but in all situations. He never left them.

From comprehensive knowledge he knew why and how he had to guide. His deep knowledge enabled him to touch students to the quick, to make his mark with a few words, even a single penetrating comment. Always present, he was a role model for all circumstances.

He was demanding. He set a tone: *Slobodka is for workers.* This was neither preached nor enforced.

It was assumed.

The Alter worked incessantly; so would his students have to.

Under the press of crisis, the Alter adjusted his Musar approach, but not his level of demand. Slobodka passed through three major periods of rebellion, the first in 1897, when a general attack on the Musar movement penetrated Slobodka and split it in two, "Knesses Beis Yisrael" under the Alter, and "Knesses Beis Yitzchak," later under Rabbi Boruch Ber Leibowitz; the second in 1903, when those Slobodka students opposed to Musar sat apart, *en bloc*, on one side of the *beis hamidrash*; and in 1904 to 1905, when winds of Russian revolution reached into the yeshiva.

The Alter rose above the attacks on Slobodka, waiting out storms, talking with students, winning many of them back, persisting in his *derech* or orientation.

But he also altered his *derech*, stressing less the Divine penalties for failure to live up to the Divine demands, more the "greatness of man"—*gadlus ha'adam*—the immensity of human potential, the latent spiritual heights awaiting actualization, the ability to sidestep penalty by leaping up the rungs of intellectual (Talmudic) and personal (Musar) growth.

In setting forth these goals, the Alter was demanding. He told students they could achieve. He knew how to say it—directly and indirectly, positively and by reproof—and he knew exactly what each student could attain.

This was the Alter's inexplicable genius.

But that he set high goals, for himself and his students, that he demanded work—there was nothing mysterious here.

Musar, to the Alter, meant taking Hashem's commandments with the seriousness that only Eternity—Truth—Redemption—could command.

The Alter seethed with a vision.

More: he imparted it.

Then there was Rabbi Moshe Mordechai Epstein, one of the remarkable prodigies of the Volozhin yeshiva. Rabbi Moshe Mordechai and his brother-in-law, Rabbi Isser Zalman Meltzer, were selected by the Alter to be the two main Talmudic lecturers in Slobodka in 1894, but only three years later Rabbi Isser Zalman left to head the new yeshiva in Slutsk.

Rabbi Moshe Mordechai, 17 years the Alter's junior, quickly matured into a yeshiva dean of commanding intellect, lucid exposition, and unwavering dedication. It is one thing to inspire a student, as did the Alter; it is something else to channel inspiration into extensive acquisition of Talmudic knowledge, as did Rabbi Moshe Mordechai.

He was Slobodka's intellectual channel.

For thirty years, 1897 to 1927, Rabbi Moshe Mordechai and the Alter meshed completely. A team, they built Slobodka.

Rabbi Moshe Mordechai produced five volumes, *Levush Mordechai*, that rank among the most profound Torah novellae of this century.

Rabbi Moshe Mordechai's method or "*derech* in learning" was multifaceted. It linked the logical analysis taught by Rabbi Chaim Soloveitchik in Volozhin to a style of *beki'ut* or comprehensive analysis that Rabbi Moshe Mordechai developed on his own. To him, the comprehensive knowledge of every "out-of-the-way" source in Chazal—*Yerushalmi*, *Tosefta*, *midreshei halachah*, and *mishnayos* in *Taharos*, for example—served the purpose of logical analysis. In his study of the Babylonian Talmud, Rabbi Moshe Mordechai used his comprehensive knowledge to provide a prooftext, a term, or an insight that verified a logical hypothesis. To Rabbi Moshe Mordechai, *sevarah*, logic, and *beki'ut*, wide knowledge, were not two methods of Talmud study. They were two parts of one method.

Rabbi Moshe Mordechai had a universal appeal because any intellectual inclination could find support in his method, especially since he wrote and lectured with clarity and ease. A student with a penetrating mind, wishing to plumb the logical depths of any Talmudic passage; a student with a curious mind, wishing to range widely among Talmudic sources; a student with a special interest in a particular branch of Talmudic literature; a student with an overarching mind like Rabbi Moshe Mordechai's itself—any student could proceed under the masterful eye of Rabbi Moshe Mordechai. A yeshiva dean with a many sided method, he appealed to a variety of students. Hence the diversity of brilliance that characterized the great *talmidei chachamim* of Slobodka.

Diversity: Slobodka produced that rare scholar whose Talmudic expertise was so thorough and sound that he could investigate the history of Talmudic literature without distorting it—a scholar such as Rabbi Yechiel Yaakov Weinberg. Slobodka produced a pedagogue such as Rabbi Yitzchak Aizik Sher; a communal leader such as Rabbi Yaakov Kaminecki; a pietist such as Rabbi Yaakov Moshe Lesin; a literary stylist such as Rabbi Yosef Zev Lipovitz. Slobodka produced Rabbi Avraham Eliyahu Kaplan, scholar, poet, and composer who strengthened Talmudic study in Western Europe; and Rabbi Avraham Grodzinski, *mashgiach* in Slobodka who produced one of the Musar movement's most profound works, *Toras Avraham* (and who bequeathed one of the movement's most effective teachers in his son-in-law, Rabbi Shlomo Wolbe).

Rabbi Moshe Mordechai produced lifelong diligence in Talmudic study without stifling the Alter's cultivation of individual aspirations. With the Alter, Rabbi Moshe Mordechai produced Slobodka.

Of course, it took the Alter's genius to recognize the pedagogic advantage to Rabbi Moshe Moredechai's method. It took the Alter's self-effacement to allow Rabbi Moshe Mordechai the freedom to develop it. What was the Alter's secret? The more I see the diversity of its fruits, the less I fathom it.

"Above all," wrote Rabbi Dov Katz, "the Alter was astonishing in his mastery of all books of *Tanach*, all their commentaries, all *aggados* of *Chazal*. Virtually nothing in them was hidden from him. He overflowed with their ideas. From morning to night, for 50 years, he elucidated byways of thought and Musar. He never prepared a lecture; it all flowed as if spontaneously. He cited, innovated, added and burnished, without pause. There was no subject in Torah he did not touch, no subject he did not give extra weight with his interpretation. If his words had been transcribed, they would have filled tens of volumes.

"He would cite, he would deepen, further and further; he would create whole systems of thought.

"Few understood him; those who did, did not do so fully. When his students reviewed his talks, he would frequently reprimand them, saying they did not grasp his point, and then, with his elaboration, he would layer it, deepen it, layer after layer, until it seemed to be another idea altogether. The mind wearied.

"From this you see how great the Alter was in depth of thought, in knowledge of G-d; how splendid was his person.

"Now, besides depth of thought, the Alter was blessed with powerful emotion. He himself came to great inspiration during his talks. Although he struggled to hold it in, he did not always succeed. Sometimes his face turned ecstatic, his forehead shone, his eyes sparked. It was clear, he had turned entirely to self-transcendence, to ecstasy.

"Mainly this occurred on Sabbath evening—Friday night—in his talks on the holiness of Sabbath, and on the delights of spiritual life. More than once we sensed that his tears—tears of the heart—choked him to such an extent that sometimes he had to bite his lips, stub his finger, to hold them in. Sometimes he even had to get up from his table, to halt his talk in the middle.

"The Alter criticized passion and tears which originated in weeping or melancholy humming—such were the eye's tear, not the heart's tear. He said that even Reb Yisrael Salanter never wished to turn Musar study into an impassioning of the soul by a 'melancholy and sad voice' [as Reb Itzele Peterburger maintained]. But when it was depth of thinking and clarity of ideas that generated passion and tears, they were of great worth, said the Alter. They were a good sign.

"The Alter took to ecstasy in prayer also. Virtually no voice of his was heard, no motion was detected, but one who looked into his face saw that it burned, as a scorching flame. In special prayers, such as *shema* or the 13 attributes of G-d, he emitted a great noise, calling out in immense passion, his whole body trembling."

The Alter created great disciples because he knew that first he had to, and did, create himself.

Chevron, 1929.

Arabs rampaged, knifed, murdered nearly 60 Jews.

Two students in Yeshivas Chevron—founded by the Alter in 1924—lay on the floor of the yeshiva. One bled profusely. One was merely dazed. The bleeding student saw that he was mortally wounded. He had a few seconds, perhaps a minute or two, to live. Life was rushing out of him with each drop. He turned to his fellow student, merely dazed, and said to this effect:

"Come, get under me. Let my blood flow over you. Then you will appear dead also, and they will leave you alone."

And so it was.

With a few seconds left to live, one person—just a young student, actually—had the love, and the presence of mind, to use his very life blood to save someone else's.

This is what the Alter created.

He attained and imparted self-control, the rule of the impulses by the rational faculty so pervasive, so sober, that no desire or distraction—not even death itself—could drive the Divine demand for human kindness from the center of consciousness.

It might take years of steady, painful work on personal discipline to attain this level of kindness and control, to be the model for their imitation.

Whatever it took, the Alter did it.

But he did not show it. He hid his *avodas hamusar* or work on himself, as well as his *limmud haTorah*, study of Torah. No one was really certain how extensive the Alter's Talmudic knowledge was, as he almost never spoke in areas other than Musar, *Tanach*, and *aggadah*. Rabbi Moshe Mordechai testified that the Alter knew the entire Talmud with the commentary of *Rosh*. But more. How could the Alter have an unerring eye for future *gedolei Torah* if he could not identify authentic intellectual talent? How could he distinguish between surface brilliance and real gifts if he were not a great Talmudic scholar himself?

We ask these questions—we are reduced to speculation—because the Alter's ultimate purpose was neither to demonstrate his knowledge of Talmud nor to display his attainments in *avodas hamusar*.

The Alter's ultimate purpose was to teach and guide, to draw out the potential of others. He remains a mystery because he perfected the art of pedagogy. His every living moment, on the level of the visible, was instructional. No one could know anything about the state of his soul or the level of his knowledge because no one had to. This would have been irrelevant to the education of his students. Their progress was the focus of his attention and self-revelation, nothing else. He pushed Slobodka to a peak of perfection in turning his every waking moment to the education, the self-control and intellectual advancement, of his students. The Alter neared perfection in fulfilling his obligation in his world: the perfect education of others.

Who was the Alter of Slobodka? He was a pedagogue. The glint in his small, limpid, oh so wise eyes, uncovered greatness in others even as it covered the greatness in himself.

This, too, is imitation of Hashem. "Just as He is merciful, you, too, be merciful" (*Shabbos* 133b)... Just as He both reveals His activity and conceals His essence, you, too.

Y ou, too, can achieve spiritual exaltation.

This, the Alter's message to himself, was his message to his students. *Gadlus ha'adam*, the greatness of man, was his byword.

Man is the purpose of creation. He is the center of creation. "*See how beautiful, how rich, is all of creation,*" the Holy One, Blessed be

He, told man, "*I created it all for you*" (*Kohelet Rabbah* 7). Man is the best of creation, formed from its choicest earth (*Sanhedrin* 38a); woman is the best of man, formed from his choicest part, the rib.

> The Holy One, Blessed be He, created woman not from man's head, lest she be lightheaded; not from his eye, lest she be nosy; not from his ear, lest she be obedient; not from his mouth, lest she be garrulous; not from his heart, lest she be jealous; not from his hand, lest she be servile; not from his leg, lest she be clumsy; but from his modest place, his rib, did He create her, for even when man is unclothed this place is covered. So He could say about each and every limb of woman that He created: woman is modest. (*Bereishis Rabbah* 18)

Created from the best, created for the best, and the beautiful, man and woman can turn their lives to the morally beautiful. They *can*. For they have a soul, a spiritual essence. But even more—stressed the Alter and his disciples—the body of man and woman is itself spiritual. Man and woman have spirit and they *are* spirit. Said the Alter's son-in-law and successor as head of Slobodka in Lithuania, Rabbi Yitzchak Aizik Sher:

> Talmud (*Sotah* 12a) records: In response to Pharaoh's decree that all newborn Jewish males be cast into the Nile, Amram no longer saw a reason for Jews to bear children. Since the Jews were fated to extinction, why bear more children? He divorced his wife, whereupon all Jews did likewise. Amram's daughter challenged her father in three ways. One of them: Your decree is worse than Pharaoh's. He would remove Jewish children from this world; Amram, from the world-to-come! With that, Amram retook his wife, and so did all Israel.
>
> Rabbi Sher comments: Amram's daughter criticized her father for denying the world-to-come to children who would be killed immediately after birth. In accepting Amram's daughter's critique, Talmud regards the new-born babe, wholly without learning and *mitzvos*, as destined to the world-to-come. This can only be due to spirituality inherent in the human body, for the soul alone, before it is joined to the body, is not destined to the world-to-come. Only joined to the body can the soul reach

the ultimate goal, even if the body has not performed one single *mitzvah*. The body is inherently spiritual; the body is sacred. (*Leket Sichos Hamusar; Sanhedrin* 110b.)

Exalted in soul and body, man and woman can choose morality. They can elevate or they can corrupt. Their power of decision is unique. Only man did G-d create "just short of G-d Himself" (*Psalms* 8:6).

True, *nisma'atu hadoros*, the generations have diminished in stature—but only superficially, said the Alter. The essence remains. The reach of all previous generations is open to all. Heaven sees man as he could be. In every generation Heaven sustains the earth and its wonders, nature and its colors, and the kaleidoscope of animal life, all for man. "For me the world was created." Center of creation, creature of choice, man can still scale the heights of the spirit. He *can*, for if the generations have chosen evil, corrupting man's Divine image, pulling him down, this only means that man can now leap upward a greater distance: *gadlus ha'adam*, man is great.

He can leap upward, he can imitate his Creator. "Just as He is merciful, you, too, be merciful . . ." Now, in Hashem, the act and thought of mercy are one. The imitation of Hashem is both behavioral and intellectual, both the act of mercy and the under-standing of mercy. In both deed and mind, man imitates Hashem. Hence, in Slobodka, deep thinking accompanied righteous acting. Calculation went hand in hand with caring. In Slobodka, man and woman became the purpose, the center, the choicest of creation because they alone imitate Hashem, the Exalted One.

The achievement of greatness in Slobodka came to powerful expression in qualities such as courage, control, determination, and literary style.

Courage

When World War I broke out in 1914, Lithuania quickly became a battleground. Almost all yeshivas closed. The war found the Alter in

Germany, where he was promptly imprisoned as a foreign national. Would Slobodka close, too?

Rabbi Moshe Mordechai dared to reopen the yeshiva in Minsk. When there, too, the situation deteriorated, he, the Alter (who had since been released), and Rabbi Avraham Grodzinski moved half of the yeshiva to Kremenchug, in the Ukraine. The other half was under the leadership of Rabbi Yitzchak Aizik Sher, the Alter's son Rabbi Moshe Finkel, and Rabbi Dov Zvi Heller (father-in-law of Rabbis Grodzinski and Yaakov Kaminecki). This half tried to remain in Minsk, but after a few months it, too, moved to Kremenchug.

There, riots, plagues, pitched battles, and food shortages surrounded the Slobodka yeshiva. In one riot, gangsters took a Slobodka student hostage.They stripped him almost naked and demanded a ransom of 10,000 rubles, else he be shot. They brought him to Rabbi Moshe Mordechai's house to collect the ransom.The yeshiva dean had no money. The gangsters took the student into the street to be shot. Unarmed, unaided, Rabbi Moshe Mordechai held his head, gathered his courage, walked into the street after the terrorists, and began to shout and scream. A crowd gathered. Guns were pointed this way and that, but as the crowd grew, the terrorists dispersed.

Rabbi Moshe Mordechai had saved the life of Yitzchak Yaakov Ruderman.

Control

It was *chol hamoed*, the intermediate days of *Sukkos*, in 1926. Rabbi Moshe Finkel, the Alter's son, a Talmudic and Musar master, an instructor in Chevron, died.

Lest it adversely affect the Alter's health, the Alter's students wished to conceal the tragedy until they could consult with a Jerusalem physician, a graduate of Slobodka. In the meantime, the Alter asked to visit his son. When his students stammered, he understood.

Immediately he asked for *Orach Chaim*, the code of Jewish daily law, to investigate whether he was permitted to cry on *chol hamoed*. He knew that on Sabbath he would be permitted to cry if that would relieve his pain, for Sabbath, with its commandment of *oneg* or tranquillity, did not countenance pain. Did this apply also to *chol hamoed*, with its additional festival commandment of *simchah* or joy? Would weeping contradict the joy of the festival and thus be forbidden?[1]

The Alter could not clarify the matter immediately, so he turned to the doctor, who had arrived by then, and who himself was a Talmudic scholar. The Alter asked whether he was permitted to cry, halachically and medically.

Supreme tragedy. Supreme presence of mind. Supreme dedication to commandments of Torah, including the command to safeguard health.

The doctor took the Alter's pulse, then said that it would be best for him not to cry. Whereupon he turned silent, completely.

When the Alter was on his way to the hospital, from which the funeral would depart, he burst into tears—but only once, and only for a minute. At the hospital, waiting for the funeral to begin, he greeted all of the scholars who came to the funeral with blessings for a happy holiday, with joyous countenance. "It was the talk of Jerusalem," reported Rabbi Dov Katz.

Returning to Chevron for the remainder of *Sukkos*, the Alter rejoiced as on every other festival. Finding his wife and daughter-in-law overcome with grief, he did all he could to comfort and distract them.

In the Chevron yeshiva on *Shemini Atzeres* (also *Simchas Torah* in the Land of Israel), the customary singing and rejoicing was subdued. The Alter himself sprung to life, broke out in song, and brought the rejoicing to its normal pitch.

At the end of the day, as twilight descended into night, he repeatedly asked for the time: Was it yet time for *ma'ariv*, the evening prayer? Finally, *ma'ariv* was completed. The moment it

---

1. There is another version of the Alter's quandry, according to which he believed that to cry over the death of a great Torah scholar did supersede the festival commandment of *simchah*. But he was uncertain whether he would be crying because Rabbi Moshe Finkel was a great scholar, or because he was his son. See "The Alter And His 'Only Sons,' " a pamphlet prepared by Rabbi Shlomo Freundlich and the staff of Yeshiva Merkaz HaTorah (1983).

was—the moment the required seven day mourning period or *shiva* began—the Alter broke down in uncontrollable sobbing that lasted two hours. He mourned bitterly the entire *shiva*. "There is a time to weep, and a time to rejoice; a time to mourn, and a time to dance," and a time, always, not to confuse the two.

Determination

Rabbi Dov Katz wrote that Rabbi Yitzchak Aizik Sher added his own touch to Slobodka, a touch of "exaltedness, a beauty of demeanor, a kind of conviviality and noblility of presence." Dr. Joseph Kaminetsky, leader of Torah Umesorah for decades, told me how the kindness and warmth of Rabbi Sher paradoxically brought him pain. He had to turn down Rabbi Sher's offer to leave America to study in Slobodka, since he had to care for parents. Rabbi Chaim Elazari, a Slobodka graduate who wrote several Musar works (and who attended to the Alter, actually holding his hand the moment he died), told me how he reached Slobodka young, alone, and frightened. Rabbi Sher picked him out of the large student body and brought him straight to the prestigious eastern row of the yeshiva. There, Rabbi Sher sat young Elazari down next to him to make him feel welcome.

Rabbi Sher, regal and reachable, noble and accessible, also had a will of iron.

When Lithuania ruled that yeshivas would have to incorporate secular studies, the Alter decided to move the entire yeshiva to Chevron. No sooner had the decision been made than the rule was rescinded.

The Alter regarded the turn of events as a providential impetus to take an entire yeshiva on aliyah for the first time in at least 18 centuries. Yet he also was left with a responsibility to Europe. He had to sustain Slobodka in Lithuania. To do so, he turned the yeshiva over to Rabbis Sher and Grodzinski.

Under them, Slobodka flourished until the unspeakable atrocities of the unspeakable era, during which Slobodka—the yeshiva and the city—were reduced to rubble, and Rabbi Grodzinski, to ashes. Rabbi

Sher and his own son-in-law, Rabbi Mordechai Shulman, providentially found themselves outside Lithuania when the fury struck. They made their way to Palestine. They had nothing.

Nothing but determination to sustain the vision of Slobodka—its intellectual tradition, its pietistic purpose, its communal responsibility.

And so, in 1945, Rabbi Sher went up from Jerusalem to B'nei Brak to lay the cornerstone of "Yeshivas Slobodka," which he nurtured until his death in 1952, and which then continued to grow under his son-in-law.

Slobodka, the first Musar yeshiva, survived the Holocaust.

Literary style

Taken to its logical extreme, the Musar goal of self-effacement means that this book (or any book) on the Musar movement could not be written. Musar personalities not only do not seek to become known, they actively seek to suppress clues to their piety (not to mention recognition such as honors and publicity). Of necessity, this book is based on bits and pieces of information gathered over several years, snatched from an exchange on Purim or during a *shiva*, built from extensive personal observation, drawn from incidents recorded in books or divulged in considered conversation. It is necessary to be a sleuth, a kind of private investigator in the realm of the spiritual.

Not always does the search bear fruit. Some Musar personalities leave virtually no trace. The trackless trail is all the more inaccessible when such personalities leave no progeny.

This was Rabbi Yosef Zev Lipovitz.

Next to nothing is known about his life. He left no children. The bits and pieces about him, put into their pattern, reveal him as one of the Alter's most remarkable disciples.

He studied under the Alter in Slobodka several years and also earned high praise from Rabbi Moshe Mordechai and Rabbi Meir Simchah (author of *Or Sameach*) for his Talmudic knowledge. He married, studied under Rabbi Chaim Heller in Berlin, then went to the Land of Israel. There, he became the first to teach Talmud in the Lithuanian manner in Hebrew. When his health weakened, he and his wife opened a small restaurant in Tel Aviv. On a voluntary basis he lectured in Torah several times weekly, helped found the Heichal HaTalmud yeshiva, and later administered the finances for Ponavitch yeshiva. Born in 1889, he died in 1962.

In his case, the tell-tale clue to his greatness is literary remains. What almost every major master in the first three generations of the Musar movement did not leave behind, he did. From Reb Yisrael Salanter's first Musar talks in the 1840s all the way to the onset of World War II, Musar masters almost never published. The few significant exceptions included Reb Yisrael's few writings, Reb Itzele Peterburger's notations and brief biography of Reb Yisrael in *Or Yisrael* (1900), the Alter of Novorodock's pamphlets that later were printed as *Madregas HaAdam*, and contributions to Novorodock journals published in the 1920 and 1930s. For nearly a century—1840 to 1939—the Musar movement yielded almost no written works.

With good reason.

The point was to live Musar. "My life is my book," the Alter of Slobodka said. The point was to practice, to reach spiritual goals, to make living achievement the essence of Judaism.

A living Musar community did not have time to write. It was too occupied with self-analysis, whose results were used to devise rigorous experiments in self-effacement, self-control, and helping others. All this, with Torah study, consumed the Musar practitioners' time. To write, too? This was a distraction; at best, superfluous.

But, as noted, there were exceptions.

The most notable was Rabbi Yosef Zev Lipovitz. He was the master stylist of the Musar movement.

For Rabbi Lipovitz, his writing *was* his living. It was his Musar discipline, his self-analysis, his quest for purity. Writing was his being.

He wrote only at the end of his life. For writing then to have been the practice of Musar, it had to have been a consummation of years of *avodas Hashem*, an integration of decades of Musar study and struggle. In Rabbi Lipovitz's case, we may assume this to have been so, since his writings give evidence of inner balance, serenity, and self-effacement. Rabbi Lipovitz's writings reveal him as both humble and insightful, empty of artifice and filled with passion. Even more, they reveal him as possessor of a perspective that was comprehensive, that, as is said of the Alter himself, creatively interpreted all of *Tanach* and its numerous commentaries, as well as the numerous *aggados* of *Chazal*.

Rabbi Lipovitz was more than comprehensive, he was penetrating. A leading *talmid chacham* in Israel told me that he did not understand how to read *Chazal* until he had studied with Rabbi Lipovitz. One of the eminent living expositors of non-halachic Torah texts told me: "I do not understand the text as well as Rabbi Lipovitz."

Rabbi Lipovitz published a commentary on *Ruth*. After he died, his admirers (including Rabbi Isser Zalman Meltzer's son) published four more volumes, one in Halachah, three in Musar, all titled *Nachalas Yosef*—all rich wellsprings of wisdom.

All fixed by the power of the Alter.

"**A** small town has no change for large bills," said the Alter of Slobodka. This world is a small town. Only Eternity can fully appreciate large deeds—deeds of devotion, of *mesirus nefesh*. Only Hashem can adequately recognize *mitzvos* of truly great magnitude.

This world was a small town for the Alter of Slobodka. His eyes were fastened elsewhere. He lived for Eternity. He was above *kavod*. He was above honors and glory. He was above material satisfaction. He had Hashem's work to do; he had great disciples to create. He had the future of *klal yisrael* to ensure.

We describe his deeds. As amply, as fully, as we do, we do so inadequately. The Alter traded only in large bills. We, of this world, cannot properly appraise them. We leave the Alter as we began: a mystery.

Only Hashem can add up his deeds.

Part Five: Conclusion

Part Five

10.

The Secret

Rabbi Eliezer Ben Zion Bruk used to visit the daughter of the late Rabbi David Budnick (one of the Alter of Novorodock's seven major disciples). His daughter was seriously ill. Rabbi Bruk used to visit her—he told me—not only because it is a *mitzvah* to visit the ill, but also out of respect. Rabbi Bruk's was not a transposed respect, not a respect for her *yichus* or family standing. He visited her because he respected *her*, a *ba'alas Musar*, a female Musar master. He respected her for her own accomplishments in Musar.

Rabbi Bruk's attitude stemmed from Reb Yisrael Salanter's third letter, which obligates men and women equally to work in Musar—to ennoble character and deepen piety. This letter created the dynamics which culminated in female ba'alei Musar, such as Rebbetzin Sarah Yaffen and the daughter of Rabbi David Budnick; and in couples who worked mutually in Musar, such as the Alter of Kelm and his wife Sarah Leah, and the Alter of Novorodock and his wife Chaya.

With female ba'alei Musar, we do not find the same richness of oral tradition that we find with males. Women had few institutional outlets to sustain the evidence that all ba'alei Musar tried so hard to hide. From the Musar point of view, female ba'alei Musar were privileged: their self-effacement could be more complete, their notable deeds less noted. I suspect this accounts for our lack of knowledge of Golda Frank. Still, Musar women are more the rule than the exception, as the rule in the Musar movement is that remembrance survives unintentionally.

Were it not for Rabbi Yechezkel Sarna's stumbling upon an unknown Slobodka attic filled with papers, then noticing some in the Alter of Slobodka's handwriting, posterity would have been without the Alter's diary—a rich addition to our understanding of him.

Were it not for Rabbi Yosef Zev Lipovitz's confinement to bed, which made him publish before it was too late, posterity would have been ignorant of him.

Sometimes there is no remembrance at all. Searchers or researchers arrive after it is too late. In his work on the Musar movement, Rabbi Dov Katz sometimes names Musar figures, then regretfully adds that virtually no information about them exists.

Even when remembrance is perpetuated by design, often we are tantalized as much by what we are not told as by what we are told. Take, for example, the remembrance of the Alter of Kelm's daughter, Mrs. Nechamah Liba Broide.

The Alter wrote:

> She almost entirely changed her nature. I have seen very few like her ... We may learn something astonishing from her, in the sense of Ibn Ezra's comment (Numbers 6:2): *Every person wishes to satiate his lust, except for the person who astonishes—who separates from his lust.*

The nature of every person is that which is inborn, except for the person [such as my daughter] who can create a new nature—this is astonishing.

Mrs. Broide knew her father's Musar teachings thoroughly. After the death of her husband, Rabbi Zvi Broide, people came to her for counsel in matters of Musar. The remembrance of Rabbi Moshe Rosenstein, *mashgiach* in Lomz:

> [Of the four masters to whom I owe gratitude], the fourth is the daughter of our master and teacher, Rabbi Simcha Zisl, the widow of our teacher Rabbi Zvi Broide, the woman who is great in wisdom, knowledge, fear of Heaven, and sterling qualities, just like one of the great disciples of our master and teacher: Mrs. Nechamah Liba, may she live a long life, about whom I am too insignificant to recite her praise.
>
> When I lived in Kelm and spent much time in her household, I had the opportunity to study her path in wisdom and fear of Heaven, and her good deeds. We all learned much from her since everything she did was based on the wisdom of our master and teacher.
>
> She was not only his daughter.
>
> She was his great and honored disciple.
>
> We learned piety and character from her, and also were the recipients of many favors from her. Her memory will not be erased from my heart forever.

When her husband Rabbi Zvi Broide was ill and then when he died, before his time, her behavior resembled that of the Alter of Slobodka, facing the death of his own son, before his time. Rather than break down, Mrs. Broide bore her grief silently, and used her energy to give strength to others. She worked to insure that no class or custom in the yeshiva was interrupted. On Purim that year, with the entire yeshiva overcome with grief, she herself told the student body to rejoice as on any other Purim.

We know just enough about Mrs. Broide to frustrate us. We know that this *ba'alas Musar* created a new nature; we do not know how.

We know still less about the Alter of Kelm's daughter Rachel Gittel. We know, simply, that once she had to undergo major surgery and refused to take anesthetic. When her life was in danger, she wanted to remain clear-headed. During the entire operation she gave no voice to her pain.

Facing death, she had to face Hashem, not pain.

The purity of spirit or devotion to humanity of *ba'alei Musar* is confirmed by the way they died—at least those about whose death we have information. Honoring humility, seeing pleasure in anonymity—perceiving preciousness in every living moment—*ba'alei Musar* disclose their authenticity most poignantly in face of death.

• Reb Yisrael Salanter spent his last hours quieting the fears of his frightened watchman, who dreaded spending the night with a corpse.

• Rabbi Elinka Kartinga requested a *minyan* to recite *mishnayos* around his deathbed, that he depart in purity, but he added a proviso: If the death chamber turned out to be small, the *minyan* should be sacrificed lest it make the room stuffy and hasten death, even by an instant. No one should be guilty of that for the sake of his desire to depart in purity.

• The Alter of Kelm sent his clothes to the cleaners a few days before he died. The poor to whom he bequeathed his clothes should receive them pressed and clean.

• The Alter of Novorodock saw no grounds on which to exempt himself from joining volunteers who treated his disciples during a typhus epidemic. He treated them, contracted the disease, and died.

• The Alter of Slobodka, on his deathbed, was mistakenly given a spoonful of liquor, and choked. His ministering student fled in horror and shame. Critical moments passed; the Alter regained his breadth. He noticed that the student was absent and called for him. "You made me happy," the Alter said, to set him at ease. "At first I panicked, but after it passed I saw it was nothing, and was very happy." Shortly thereafter the Alter lapsed into unconsciousness, never to recover.

• A Slobodka disciple, fatally wounded by rioting Arabs and laying in his own blood, had the presence of mind to save another's life by asking that his own soon-to-be lifeless corpse be pulled over his friend, who would become blood-soaked and play dead.

• Rabbi Daniel Movshovitz, standing alongside a death pit with guns pointed at him, had the presence of mind to compress his entire knowledge of Torah into a summary of the Laws of Martyrdom.

The Musar love of the worthy life prevented death's invasion of the spiritual domain prior to its invasion of the physical domain. Ba'alei Musar lived with such zest for the holy—the ethically right, the spiritually elevated—that no decay or despair set in before the moment of death. In flight from vainglory their entire lives, in flight toward *mitzvos* every moment, Musar masters knew how to live every moment, even under the shadow of death. With their cultivation of self-eclipse and their training in the holy, they knew how to transcend self-doubt at life's end, how to remain open then, as always, to cultivating Torah's values in word or deed.

A striking example of living within .Torah selflessly and self-effacingly is communicated by Rabbi Yechiel Yaakov Weinberg's remembrance of Rabbi Shlomo Zalman Dulinsky.

Rabbi Shlomo Zalman Dulinsky's father mastered the entire Talmud; his nephew was Rabbi David Hacohen, the nazirite of Jerusalem; his cousin was Rabbi Dov Katz. Reb Shlomo Zalman himself was a disciple of the Alter of Kelm. The Alter of Slobodka hired Reb Shlomo Zalman in 1900 as the younger Musar figure in Slobodka, then urged him to move to the Mir yeshiva, in 1907, to win it to the way of Musar.

In everything he did Reb Shlomo Zalman was successful. His demeanor was pleasant. He influenced others with conviviality and personal concern. An extant picture shows him to be handsome and commanding, also humble and inward, his eyes both serene and searching, his dress immaculate.

He embodied the spirit and dignity—relentless self-scrutiny and nobility—of his background and training.

He contracted a terminal illness in 1908, suffered three years, then died at about 40.

So little remembrance remains.

He hid himself in the extreme. This friendly inspirer of youth, convivial confidant of future scholars, affable model for lay people, lived a separate life in *avodas Hashem*, even as he mixed easily in company.

So little remembered—the time he skipped dangerously across melting ice to do a stranger a favor; the time he spontaneously recited the Priestly blessing for a wagon driver whom he did not even know, as the driver set out on a dangerous journey; the rabbinical positions he turned down so as not to become a public figure; the silence he maintained on all but sacred matters during *Elul*—so little remembered.

But a picture emerges.

Reb Shlomo Zalman lectured convincingly about transcending selfishness because he himself transcended. He taught the Musar ideal of living as if one were a recluse, an unknown, because he himself lived that way. He expected students to be open with him and they were, because he was open with them. Wishing them to share, he shared. Reserving his most earnest emotions for Hashem, he yet knew how to seek and to be a friend. He mastered the gesture of togetherness and of separation. Of aloneness before the Alone.

He mastered purity.

If he cried, it could be release of pure tears—not search for pity. If he inspired, it could be communication of his inner flame, not manipulation of others'. If he suffered, it could be without compromise of joyful countenance, even without compromise of inner serenity. If he died, it could elicit immense sorrow: pains of purity, Rabbi Weinberg's "Just One Tear." This eulogy describes Reb Zalman Dulinsky's integration of inner secrecy, satisfaction, and service of others:

> One tear on his bier.
> *"Now there was found in* [a little city, besieged by a great king,] *a poor wise man, and he delivered the city with his wisdom, yet no person remembered that poor man"* (Ecclesiastes 9:15).
> Reb Zalman—wondrous was the man, wondrous his life. He and his life—his entirety—were *Secret*. An

inscrutable secret. No one knew him in his life; all the more so in his death.

Separate was the man, separate in life—singular, without friend.

He knew well how to reduce, contract himself, to make himself insignificant, literally to compress himself—his being—that no one recognize him, that he elicit no perceptive glance.

People passed him by, noticed nothing, saw nothing. But how could they notice? "The *Secret*." He was a secret, inscrutable, empty of anything contrary to his integrity. A master of *Secret*, he knew how to hide it within, how to protect it from perceptive glance. In this he was an artist, almost a magician. He revealed himself in every appropriate context, he was simplicity incarnate. And yet: how distant, o so distant, he was from us.

Reb Zalman! One tear on your bier.

Do you weep with me, readers? Heaven forbid.

Do not weep for this dead man, since his entire desire: self-eclipse. Do not agitate his bier with tears that never overcame him, unless as libations, sacred libations on the altar of Hashem.

Do not judge him! No. Do not judge: his life was sate with joy and love of Hashem, protesting-rejecting your judgment.

Did you know him? No? Why did you not know this wondrous *Secret* who walked among you? His name rang no bell. No tag hung from his neck.

What was he and who was he? A rabbi? No. A Talmud lecturer? No.

What was he?—*A flame*. Yes, a searing flame, this wondrous man. With a wick woven, spun, from the vessels of his burning heart, he kindled the light in the heart of the youth.

This great master of the *Secret* knew the secret of inspiration. He knew it well, as did no one else, working wonders in the soul of the youth.

And now, the wick is severed, the flame extinguished, the *Secret* —secreted away.

Did he leave anything behind—a mere pittance? No! His bequest was great.

Tens and hundreds of disciples encircling the bier . . .

and weeping? No. He decreed that no one weep. But they remember, and cause his name to be remembered, with exultation, with quivering, with sacred reverence. And when his name is pronounced by his disciples they hasten to vow: Let us preserve, as the apple of our eye, the light he kindled within us.

Reb Zalman! Your fire is hidden, preserved in the soul of the youth. Your words are sealed, etched on the hearts of youth whom you nurtured. No, they shall not waver on the threshold of the journey, neither shall they fall back. They will travel forward; the long journey is before them.

My life is narrowed for your demise, my brother Reb Zalman, since you brought me such delight. But no, I shall not speak, shall not reveal the *Secret*. Heaven forbid, Reb Zalman.

But it presses so, my hurt; it strangles so. Just one tear!

The eulogist, Rabbi Yechiel Yaakov Weinberg, needed to cry; Reb Shlomo Zalman did not. Suffering, watching his life slip away, Reb Shlomo Zalman took his meaning from *mitzvos*, from the anonymity and hence purity he discovered in doing the will of Hashem. He needed no recognition: who could top recognition from Hashem? Of course, it hurt to lose the life he loved, to lose the opportunity to perform more *mitzvos*, to become still closer to Hashem and more devoted to humanity. It hurt, but it was secondary. The purity with which he imbued his relationship with Hashem not only surpassed the normal needs for pleasure and praise that gnaw at those less practiced in Musar, but even surpassed the thirst for spiritual growth. Approaching the moment of oneness with Hashem, he was at one with himself. And so, the eulogist wished to cry (quite naturally), while the deceased dropped no tear. He was content with his *Secret*. Rabbi Jechiel Yitzchak Perr summarized all this years ago in a moving eulogy of a *mashgiach* in Novorodock, Rabbi Yisrael Movshovitz. Rabbi Movshovitz lost his family in the Holocaust, and Rabbi Perr described his secret as follows:

> . . . a picture emerges. A picture of a man who didn't have to cry in the presence of others in order to grieve for a never-to-be-healed wound. A man who didn't have to be

acknowledged as a righteous person in order to be righteous. A man who had no need to see the reflection of his greatness in the eyes of others in order to be great. A man so sure of all he was that he didn't need public recognition to strengthen his conviction.

Strength of conviction.

Meaning, of course, not only spiritual conviction, not only belief; meaning the entire range of human emotion, integrity, and knowledge. Reb Yisrael Movshovitz's conviction was, in current parlance, "together"; in traditional Musar parlance, *shalem*, harmonious and whole.

The death of Rabbi Nachum Zev Broide, son of the Alter of Kelm, brought to an almost unbelievable peak the strength of conviction, understood in its broadest sense, that a *ba'al Musar* could attain. Rabbi Nachum Zev's self-awareness, self-control, and serenity were so firm that he seemed able to measure his last moments, to know precisely how to prepare for his own demise, and his survivors' needs. In fact, the two were one; the preparation of himself, and of his survivors, were cut from one cloth, projected from one conviction.

• So that his wife and crippled daughter would not suffer physically at his funeral, he himself ordered a carriage for them, for the day of his death.

• To share his best insights on death, he lectured on "the day of death is better than the day of birth" the night before he died.

• To safeguard his family members, he warned them to take special care in eating fish on the Sabbath following his death, lest from sorrow they pay insufficient attention to the bones and choke.

• To be humble and honest, he commanded that his eulogy be limited to one single praise: that he had had the will to draw near to *emunah*, faith in Hashem.

In Kelm circles they used to say: It was worthwhile to come from afar to see Rabbi Nachum Zev's death, to learn how to die.

When life is exemplary — lived to its fullest, its holiest — exemplary death suffuses life with meaning, even as exemplary life empties death of dread.

But make no mistake. In Musar, neither is meaning in life derived solely from death, even exemplary death, nor is death to be desired, even death empty of dread and full of faith. Meaning in life is derived from life; and life, not death, is to be sought in every way. The way *ba'alei Musar* died is significant because it is the way they always lived: in thirst for life, for growth in Torah.

They would do anything to escape death.

Except violate their integrity.

Which is why we have instances of martyrdom, literally, in the case of Kelm's Rabbi Movshovitz; virtually, in the case of Reb Yozel, the Alter of Novorodock.

We also have instances of escape from death precisely because *ba'alei Musar* refused to violate their integrity. Sacrificial dedication to principle—purity of spirit and devotion to humanity—ended in their rescue by *hashgachah*, Providence. Of course, they dedicated themselves to principle not from knowledge that Providence would reward them. They had no way of knowing this, nor did they expect it.

But it often happened that way.

There is the case of Rabbi Gedalyah Dessler.

Rabbi Dessler, brother of Kelm's leader Rabbi Reuven Dov Dessler, found himself in World War I in Gomel, on the border between White Russia and the Ukraine. This was the city in which Novorodock and other Musar yeshivas flourished during the war. It was the city, and the time, in which spirituality flourished only in sacrificial coping with food shortages, shifting political authority, and streams of refugees.

Rabbi Gedalyah Dessler hired an impoverished Russian student to tutor his daughters. To him, a disciple of Kelm, secular study in proper context was advisable.

One day his family noticed a valuable golden goblet missing. Suspicion fell on the Russian tutor.

Rabbi Dessler confronted him. He tearfully admitted the truth. He needed money for tuition, he said; he had pawned the goblet, and intended to return it.

He deeply regretted taking it.

Rabbi Dessler fired him.

But he did not wish to embarrass him. Even him, a thief, he did not wish to embarrass.

So he told no one why he dismissed him.

And he did something else: he continued to pay the tutor's wages, just as though nothing had happened. Without wages, the student would not be able to continue his schooling. Rabbi Dessler did not want him to suffer.

Much later, when the Communists were in power, Rabbi Dessler was arrested for the "crime" of owning a typewriter or some such. He was tried, condemned to death, and taken away to await execution.

His wife knocked on all the doors, pulled all the strings. We know how much good that does in Communist Russia.

She was desperate.

One day, running from this office to the next, trying to seek amnesty for her husband, she ran into her daughter's former tutor.

He heard the story.

A hardened Communist now, he remembered Rabbi Dessler's *chesed*, his lovingkindness.

He pulled out all the stops.

In a position of authority now, he traveled to the prison in which Rabbi Dessler was held. He falsified the execution list so that it read as if Rabbi Dessler had already been killed. Then he smuggled Rabbi Dessler and his family out of Russia.

He saved his life.

All because a *ba'al Musar* had once done a kindness, completely unasked for, even undeserved, to prevent a human being from embarrassment and deprivation.

This is the Musar dedication to life—the life worth living—the life of consideration for human beings. With his rescue by a Russian agent of Providence, Rabbi Dessler received what he infinitely cherished: his own life.

The life worth living is not just in stories from the past. The Musar movement is not just a memory, deserving of remembrance. A ba'al Musar is generated not just by spiritual conditions that no longer exist.

The main spiritual condition of the ba'al Musar is his own soul. Creating it himself, he relies primarily on himself, not on others, to foster an atmosphere favorable to his soul-work. Creating himself, the ba'al Musar lives not just in generations past.

He is Rabbi Yosef Zundel Salanter, also Rabbi Yehudah Leib Nekritz; the *Maggid* of Kelm, also Rabbi Yitzchak Orlansky; Rabbi Naftali Amsterdam, also Rabbi Yaakov Lesin.

And also: Rabbi Yosef David Epstein.

On the streets of Brooklyn, one will pass him by. He makes no effort to project himself. In discussion, one hears nothing of his life or history. But here is a ba'al Musar with an encyclopedic Talmudic mind, with what the Alter of Kelm called the prerequisite to creativity.

On this foundation, Rabbi Epstein sifts the vast Talmudic literature for Musar topics that no one has ever quite viewed the way he does. In contemporary Musar books, he has collected Talmudic teachings on peace, marriage, and counsel.

To what lengths must one go to pursue peace? What supersedes the pursuit, justifying debate or even dispute?

What are the obligations of husband to wife, of wife to husband?

To what lengths must one go to give sound advice, and to avoid misleading someone, even implicitly?

Such is Rabbi Epstein's Musar creativity, which follows the orientation of Rabbi Avraham Grodzinski, the profound *mashgiach* in Slobodka. Rabbi Grodzinski, like Reb Yisrael Salanter and the Chafetz Chaim before him and Rabbi Epstein after him, identified ethical areas of Halachah. He tried to root the Musar emphasis on human relations in Halachah itself, thereby adding concrete obligation to Torah's nurture of human sensitivity.

It takes a humble soul to assume a large responsibility. The responsibility Rabbi Epstein has assumed—to develop latent Musar teachings in hitherto unseen directions—springs from his long training in Talmud and Musar. The effort stretches back to his years in the Mir yeshiva in Shanghai, and before that in Poland, in which his soul-work on Musar was a model effort, even then.

No one will ever learn any of this from Rabbi Epstein himself. He will not trumpet his achievements; this goes against his grain. He has internalized the teachings of Musar, taking them from theory to practice, from books to life.

Another thing one will never learn from him: his own guidance by Providence, his own miracles in escape from the inferno of Europe, in trek across wastes of Siberia to Shanghai. The insatiable thirst for life, and the sacrificial dedication to principle, have blessed our generation, too, with *ba'alei Musar*.

O ur generation, too.
Creating his own soul, becoming both seedbed and realization of his own Musar: no one fits the description better than Rabbi Gershon Liebman. I have heard tales of his sheer force of will; I have seen him only twice. My notes read:

"On the short side; round head; bald; not fully sprouted beard. Reminds me of Rabbi Orlansky—that *simchah*, that twinkle— knowing twinkle—in the eyes.

"Energy: looks down at the ground when he speaks, whole body bending back and forth. No need to be demonstrative; the raw power is there, all about him. No wonder he could defy Nazis.

"No raised voice, no yelling and screaming, but a great *hisorerus*, arousal. His whole being: passion. Interrupts himself often. The silences speak as loudly as the words echo softly.

"Speaks only five to seven minutes. Needn't say much; he acts on what he says; everyone knows this. Few words, few points; his finishing is his silence—his time for action."

Rabbi Gershon Liebman: a man who makes a mockery of referring to Novorodock Musar in past tense. A man who founded a Novorodock network in France after the war. A man who disdains possessions, flees from *kavod* or honor, sizes up situations very quickly: will they hurt, or help, *avodas Hashem*? If they will help, *act*.

Rabbi Liebman travels everywhere: morning in Paris, afternoon in Jerusalem, back again. Then New York. Everything for a sacred purpose; everything utterly without self-aggrandizement. In France, he rebuilt the Novorodock aspiration.

He survived the war, like everyone else, with only his life. No matter. A *ba'al bitachon* needs no resources; Hashem gives them—if only one trusts utterly.

Rabbi Liebman trusts utterly.

Through him, one imagines the Alter of Novorodock: a cultivation of sacred consciousness so total that nothing penetrates unless it nurtures *avodas Hashem*. Rabbi Liebman: a radical purification of vision.

My notes:

"Broken up—crying—not afraid to show emotion [this was the memorial gathering on Rabbi Nekritz's first *yahrzeit*]. It's tough to keep himself under control. Swaying—weeping slightly—hitting the lectern. No grand gestures, no logical ending. Just walks away. Said what he had to say. Said it, and left."

The Novorodock fire.

To do. To make a point, then *to do*. No extraneous activity, no superfluous gesture—even a single one would amount to *bittul Torah*, nullification of consciousness from Torah. A *ba'al Musar* wastes not even a single moment, loses not a single opportunity, however small, to serve Hashem: to think in Torah, or to act.... a few hours, and Rabbi Liebman is back to Paris.

Creating his own soul.

Musar: what is its definition?

It all boils down to this. When you see a *ba'al Musar*, you see a different specimen of humanity. You see an exquisite sensitivity to people, a heightened spirituality before Hashem. You see a person reaping the fruits of steady, strenuous work.

Work on himself.

To harvest, a farmer needs to have tilled, sown, and irrigated.

He needs to have worked.

To paint a masterpiece, an artist needs to have studied line and color, to have tried, erred, practiced, and persisted, and to have imagined a new reality.

He needs to have worked.

A *ba'al Musar* is a farmer whose field is himself, an artist whose canvas is himself. A *ba'al Musar* tills and sows, shapes and imagines, practices and persists, to create himself—a new human being.

More humane.

More holy.

More in the image of G-d than he would be without working on himself.

Or herself.

In life—every moment—the *ba'al Musar* works.

To learn to live, to learn to die.

To extract from Hashem's blueprint for life—the Torah—every point of meaning.

For mind.

For behavior.

For duties of the heart, and duties of the limbs.

Musar kindles a light. It transmits an illumination. It opens every individual to hidden powers within him—powers for kindness, holiness, beauty, and knowledge.

Musar holds up role models:

In kindness: Reb Shraga Feivel Frank, delivering groceries to the poor at midnight, secretly; an impoverished Novorodock disciple, slipping pennies in the shoe of a comrade, secretly; Reb Nachum Zev Broide, bringing kosher food, good cheer, and expert advice to the sick, regularly.

In holiness: Reb Itzele Peterburger, Reb Abramchik Tanis, and Reb Binyamin Zilber, ever more deeply in fear of Divine judgment, in awe of Divine majesty; Reb Leizer Gordon, ever more deeply in love with study of Torah.

In beauty: Rabbi Yosef Zev Lipovitz, in the understanding and the style he brought to, and derived from, Biblical and modern Hebrew.

In knowledge: Reb Yisrael Salanter, in knowledge of the human psyche; Rabbi Moshe Mordechai Epstein, in knowledge of Talmud; the Alter of Slobodka, in knowledge of prodigies; the Alter of Novorodock, in knowledge of a generation; Rabbi Shlomo Zalman Dulinsky, in knowledge of himself.

Musar opens the eye to a palace. Rabbi Shmuel Fundiler, colleague of Rabbi Lipovitz and fellow disciple of the Alter of Slobodka, offered a parable:

> Musar is like a match—a fleeting flame—lit in a palace. With the palace's lights switched off, its splendor is unseen and even harmful, as residents trip over rich furnishings, vessels, and ornaments. But with a match, the way to the light switch is revealed. One flips it and illuminates the palace continuously.

Musar is the flame showing the way to the light of Torah that illuminates our palatial residence: the world of Hashem and the soul of man.

They are the splendor.

The way to illuminate them is to light the match, to engage in Musar—*to work on oneself.*

This is the definition:

Musar is to work on oneself in order to achieve strength of conviction: honesty and helpfulness before people, holiness and humility before Hashem, self-knowledge and self-effacement before oneself.

All within Torah.

In life. In death.

Always.

No matter what the circumstance.

Always: with joy, *simchah shel mitzvah.*

And always: with awe.

With *sod Hashem lirei'av*, "the *Secret* of Hashem belongs to those who fear Him."